50 Ways to Help
Save the Earth

50 Ways

Save

REBECCA BARNES-DAVIES

to Help the Earth

HOW YOU
AND YOUR CHURCH
CAN HELP
MAKE A DIFFERENCE

WJK WESTMINSTER
JOHN KNOX PRESS
LOUISVILLE • KENTUCKY

© 2009 Rebecca Barnes-Davies

1st edition
Published by Westminster John Knox Press
Louisville, Kentucky

09 10 11 12 13 14 15 16 17 18—10 9 8 7 6 5 4 3 2 1

www.wjkbooks.com

Scripture quotations from the New Revised Standard Version of the Bible
are copyright © 1989 by the Division of Christian Education of the
National Council of the Churches of Christ in the U.S.A. and are used by permission.
Scripture quotations from the NRSV have been adapted for inclusive language.

Book design by Drew Stevens
Interior Illustrations: Teri Kays Vinson
Cover design by designpointinc.com

Library of Congress Cataloging-in-Publication Data

Barnes-Davies, Rebecca J.
   50 ways to help save the earth : how you and your church can make a
difference / Rebecca J. Barnes-Davies.
      p.   cm.
   ISBN 978-0-664-23370-9 (alk. paper)
   1. Global warming—Religious aspects—Christianity. 2. Environmental
protection—Religious aspects--Christianity. I. Title.
   BR115.G58b37 2009
   261.8'8—dc22

                                                          2009001888

PRINTED IN THE UNITED STATES OF AMERICA

∞ The paper used in this publication meets the minimum requirements
of the American National Standard for Information Sciences—
Permanence of Paper for Printed Library Materials, ANSI Z39.48-1992

Westminster John Knox Press advocates the responsible use of our natural resources. The text
paper of this book is made from 30 percent postconsumer waste.

Acknowledgments

I give thanks to God for my family—who early on instilled the values of conserving resources, recycling, gardening, and being content with "enough"; for my beloved life partner, Peter, who has faithfully accompanied me on this eco-justice journey, compassionately incorporating changes into our life; and for dear children, Alexis and Brian, whose love for the outdoors and delight in exploring helps me enjoy God's creation in a whole new way.

I cannot express enough appreciation for my colleagues in Presbyterians for Restoring Creation, who showed me how to combine environmental passion with Christian faith, as well as for a presbytery network of Stewardship of Creation Educators, the PCUSA Environmental Justice Office, the Eco-Justice Working Group of the National Council of Churches, the PCUSA Peacemaking Program, the PCUSA Hunger Program, and all those alongside whom I have learned to trust my call to care for creation—not by mastering science but by trusting intuitive concern, discovering a Christian environmental ethic, and articulating an eco-justice theology.

For their original brainstorming as well as ongoing input on the draft of this book I would like to thank Peter Barnes-Davies, Andrew Kang Bartlett, Adam Fischer, Melanie Hardison, and particularly my ever-faithful editor David Maxwell. I needed their expertise and wisdom to shape this book, and I could not (and would not) have done it without them!

To the people and congregations highlighted in this book, and to all those unnamed who have inspired me throughout the years, I give thanks for their faithful work and incredible witness! I am grateful for the stories they shared with me personally, as well as the ones I came across while doing Web research or while working with these wonderful organizations: Presbyterians for Restoring Creation, the National Religious Partnership for the Environment, Earth Ministry, the Eco-Justice Programs of the National Council of Churches of Christ in the U.S.A., and Eco-Justice Ministries.

Contents

Introduction

There is no simple checklist of either fifty, or a hundred, or a thousand foolproof ways to save the earth. If only it were that easy! The truth is that we alone cannot save the Earth. But we are called to help in God's ongoing saving work in the world. This is our task: to learn to reshape our lives to honor rather than destroy God's creation. To participate in God's saving work will be an ever-unfolding journey, one that has no definable end but that is both worthwhile and absolutely vital for the future of the planet.

If you are able to make it through all fifty ways, you will have been transformed, and you will have drastically transformed the world around you for the better. But this will not mean that you have permission to stop acting, learning, and changing your life. Instead, this guide outlines fifty ways you, your local community, and your congregation can *begin* to positively influence the outcome of climate change and enjoy participation in a vital part of Christian discipleship.

Why climate change? This book focuses on climate change as a lens to see the ways human activity is degrading the earth. If we are to help save the Earth, we must work to save it from ourselves! We recognize that global warming is one of the most serious effects humans have had on God's creation. In order to restore and protect the Earth, we must act to curb climate change.

Why fifty ways? While there are certainly more than fifty ways to care for creation, Scripture holds out the image of the fiftieth year as the jubilee year, a time when justice and Sabbath benefit the whole community: "You shall count off seven weeks of years, seven times seven years, so that the period of seven weeks of years gives forty-nine years. Then you shall have the trumpet sounded loud. . . . And you shall hallow the fiftieth year and you shall proclaim liberty throughout the land to all its inhabitants" (Lev. 25:8–10).

While we try to curb global climate change, we need to keep in mind this jubilee as our calling—the jubilee of restored relationships between people and God, between each other, and between people and all the inhabitants of creation. We must learn not only what to *do*, but how God calls us to *be*, in order to transform the dire predictions of the worst climate crisis. If we incorporate elements of rest, relationship, justice, and jubilee into our work, we will be better able to make a difference.

These fifty faithful steps to counter global warming will lead to a deepened commitment, to a habit of thoughtful living, and to practical action. Once we form this ongoing habit, the possibilities for further action are endless. None of us needs lists of "must do's" by the thousands; it is far better to get started and celebrate the effective actions we have completed, in order to then feel encouraged to take future steps.

You may notice that every seventh step in some way encourages rest or celebration. These steps are offered as a kind of observance of Sabbath—a time to rest, to celebrate God's presence, and to be shaped by the experience of simply being, of knowing that the world is holy and that the world's future is not solely up to us (thanks be to God!). God created and cares for the world, and it is helpful to rest in this knowledge. Leviticus 25 paints a portrait of the jubilee year and also describes the Sabbath or sabbatical year as a time of reconciliation and justice every seven years. Following this structure, this practical guide holds seven chapters of seven, with every seventh step focusing on the theme of Sabbath, and ends with the fiftieth step focusing on jubilee.

The Faith Response

Most mainline denominations have made strong public policy statements about climate change. Eco-justice theological and ethical writings also abound, persuading us to thoughtful action. This book offers an additional tool for your journey: a compilation of effective, concrete examples of how what we do will help change the world for good. I hope it

> ## *Terminology*
>
> **Eco-justice** is a term used in this book to communicate concerns that affect both ecological and socioeconomic issues, so that while we pursue social justice we also pursue environmental justice, and vice versa. This term was brought into use in the faith-based eco-justice movement by Presbyterian campus minister Bill Gibson.
>
> **Global climate change** may also be called global warming. The overwhelming majority of the world's scientists agree that global warming is real and that human activities have contributed to it.

helps you on your journey of resistance to, and positive interference with, climate change.

While most of us think about fighting climate change by altering how we use energy—for example, by reducing consumption, by sequestering the carbon dioxide that is a by-product of burning fossil fuels, and by supporting renewable energy—the truth is that climate change is also impacted by our interaction with *all* creation. Whereas we humans are quite good at compartmentalizing, it turns out that God's creation is not so good at pretending one part is unconnected to another. Thus, this book will offer suggestions on water, animals, land, and other ecological concerns that at first might seem unrelated to climate change. However, all of these issues both affect climate change as well as experience the effects of climate change. Likewise, some suggestions necessitate that we as people of faith reach out to scientists, public policy analysts, and others in order to learn from them. This interdisciplinary approach seeks to mimic the interconnections apparent within creation and to acknowledge that we need to use all the gifts God has provided in creation.

Consider using this book as part of a spiritual discipline. If you concentrate on one practical suggestion each week, as a way to embody prayer and devotion to God through caring for God's creation, over the course of a year you will have deepened your spiritual life and you will have made a major, meaningful difference for global climate change.

50 Ways to Help Save the Earth

The way we extract natural resources to produce energy and the way we consume the energy produced by those resources are the human-related activities most directly linked to the phenomenon we call global warming, or global climate change. Climate change comes from the greenhouse gases released into the atmosphere by the burning of fossil fuels. These greenhouse gases seriously affect both the air we breathe and the atmosphere we inhabit. Human greed and consumption of fossil fuels have precipitated this ongoing event of climate change, yet we know, thankfully, that God's desire for the flourishing of creation means that there are many alternatives to our current course.

1. ENERGY

Many of us grew up being told to turn off the lights when we leave a room or to not hold the refrigerator door open while looking for a snack. While small, these and other suggestions to conserve energy are still important. Those who have taken any of the various online "ecological footprint" quizzes have learned that it would take four to ten Earths if everyone were to consume energy the way a middle-class American does. Knowing that we only have one Earth, and that most of our energy right now comes from nonrenewable, unsustainable sources, it is essential that we learn the most important ways to reduce our personal energy consumption. Small commitments add up.

How To's

1 **Turn off lights, electronics, small appliances, and chargers** when not actively in use. Unplug those with an "always on" clock or "standby" red light. A TV set that's on for three hours and in standby for 21 hours uses about 40 percent of its energy in standby mode.[1]

2 **Replace incandescent lightbulbs** with compact fluorescent lightbulbs (CFLs) or, where available, light-emitting diodes (LEDs). CFLs use 60 percent less energy than incandescent bulbs.[2] For church use, there are many overhead and exit lights now available in LED, a highly energy-efficient lighting technology.

3 **Update your appliances and heating/cooling systems.** Buy EnergyStar electronics and appliances such as washing machines, dishwashers, and refrigerators. Recycle or dispose of old appliances in proper ways to keep heavy metals out of landfills.

4 **Insulate.** Most homes and churches could be drastically improved with insulation, weather stripping, caulking, and other means of making sure that the warm air in the cooler months or the cool air in the warmer months doesn't leak out.

5 **Recycle!** It makes a difference. An aluminum can made from a recycled can, rather than from new aluminum, saves the same amount of energy needed to run a television for three hours. Recycled paper uses only 60 percent of the energy used when making paper from new resources. Steel recycling in the United States each year saves enough energy to supply Los Angeles with nearly a decade's worth of electricity.[3]

6   **Keep it clean!** Replace filters on your furnace and on the air conditioner in your car.

7   **Adjust yourself to your environment.** Program your thermostat to not stay as warm or cool when you are not around. By moving your thermostat up two degrees in summer and down two degrees in winter, it is possible to save approximately two thousand pounds of carbon dioxide from the previous year.[4]

8   **Avoid the dryer,** especially high heats. The EPA does not rate dryers as EnergyStar compliant because all of them are huge energy consumers. Use a clothesline to dry your clothes when possible.

9   **Choose food, transportation, and housing options wisely.** The more local the food, the more fuel-efficient the transportation, and the smaller the house, the better for climate change.

10   **Mow your lawn with a reel or electric mower.** A gas-powered lawn mower puts out nasty particulate matter that you inhale, and it pollutes in one hour what it takes your car to pollute in twenty miles of driving (at best estimate)![5]

FAITH MATTERS

Make me to know your ways, O God; teach me your paths. Lead me in your truth, and teach me, for you are the God of my salvation; for you I wait all day long.

PSALM 25:4–5

How does it change our attitude about energy conservation and energy efficiency if we approach them as ways to wait on God? As God instructed humans to keep the creation in Genesis 2:15, how might caring for creation through energy conservation be a faithful following of God's paths?

Walking the Talk

In Dacula, Georgia, Hebron Baptist Church installed new energy-efficient lighting (almost a thousand new bulbs!) and not only has reduced its carbon footprint by a million pounds but is also spending $32,000 less each year in electricity bills. Congregations of many different denominations have done similar replacements and are finding that the economic and environmental payback for their investment is well worth the effort.

From the Earth Day Sunday 2008 resource "The Poverty of Global Climate Change," National Council of Churches' Eco-Justice Program.

ENERGY

While energy conservation and energy efficiency are essential steps, the development of sustainable, renewable energy sources is just as important. Renewable energy may be pricier as it first becomes available, but the more people who support sustainable energy early, the better and faster the development will happen and the more accessible that energy will become. Renewable energy sources should not be viewed as permission to continue consuming gross amounts of energy but rather should help alleviate some of the worse pressures we are placing on creation through greenhouse gas emissions.

How To's

1 **Use the source of always available renewable energy**—the sun! For instance, hang clothes to dry in the sun, open the blinds to the sun when you're cold, and close them when you're hot. Plant deciduous trees to shade exterior walls in the summer and to expose sun in the winter. Shading exterior walls by trees can reduce your air conditioning bill by 10 to 15 percent.[6]

2 **Purchase part of your energy from a green source** if your local gas and electric companies offer the option. Sign on at whatever level you can afford.

3 **Purchase carbon offsets.** For an overview of carbon offsets and some recommendations for how to choose a trustworthy source, see the Voluntary Carbon Offsets Information Portal at http://www.tufts.edu/tie/tci/carbonoffsets/index.htm.

4 **Buy solar panels** for your home or church, for water heating or electricity.

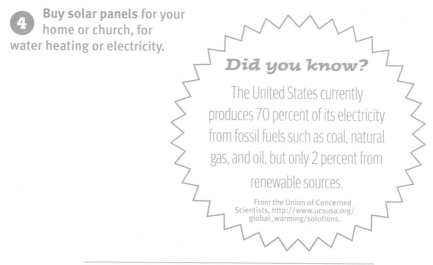

Did you know?

The United States currently produces 70 percent of its electricity from fossil fuels such as coal, natural gas, and oil, but only 2 percent from renewable sources.

From the Union of Concerned Scientists, http://www.ucsusa.org/global_warming/solutions.

Walking the Talk

Members of the Sustainability Committee of St. Paul's Episcopal Church in Chestnut Hill, Pennsylvania, have reason to be thankful. Their passion for caring for creation has been embraced by the wider congregation. This congregation's commitment has set a standard. They converted to 100 percent renewable energy for all their church needs. This striking witness not only means that they have reduced their carbon dioxide emissions by more than 60 tons a year, but it also helps church members and other congregations to imagine what is possible when one is dedicated to caring for creation. Thirty of St. Paul's households switched to green power in addition to the church's switch, heightening the impact.

From http://www.nrpe.org/profiles/profiles_vi_C_15_01.htm.

5 **Buy a solar cooker** for yourself or someone else. Sun-baked brownies are a real treat!

6 **Advocate for federal legislation** that will support research and development for renewable energy.

7 **Study renewable energy sources** that are useful in low-technology places around the world and see what mission projects your church might support in these areas.

8 **Read various opinions** about what constitutes truly sustainable energy sources. While some sources advocate for nuclear or coal as part of the sustainable energy solution, there is cause to be concerned about these options. Preference should be given to true renewable energy sources.

FAITH MATTERS

O God, you have energized the whole world, from the beginning of time to now. You give the gift of energy so that our lives may be rich and glorify you. Help us to honor the energy your Holy Spirit blows through creation and to use this energy sustainably, so that your blessings will continue to be felt for generations.

ENERGY

Sun-Baked Brownies

½ cup shortening
2 1-oz. squares unsweetened chocolate
2 eggs
1 cup sugar
1 teaspoon vanilla
¾ cup flour
½ teaspoon baking powder
½ teaspoon salt
1 cup broken walnuts

Melt shortening and chocolate together in solar cooker; cool. Beat eggs until light; stir in sugar, then chocolate mixture and vanilla. Add dry ingredients, mix well. Add nuts. Bake in greased 9-inch round dark roaster pan, covered, for one hour. Cut into squares. (Don't worry about burning the brownies—solar cooking will not burn food!)[7]

Advocate for Clean Air Laws

Another aspect of energy use and the burning of fossil fuels is air pollution. Stronger clean air laws and limits on the greenhouse gas emissions allowed from industry will go a long way toward curbing climate change and creating a healthier environment in which all can thrive. Air pollution particularly impacts children's health, causing problems such as asthma, and it is worse in lower-income communities as well as in communities of people of color. Advocacy for clean air is true eco-justice advocacy, demanding justice for the earth and for all people.

Advocate for Clean Air Laws

Walking the Talk

Members of many denominations have participated in international meetings about climate change for years. The World Council of Churches has arranged for leaders from the member communions to be present at international climate negotiations for decades. People of faith join these policy conversations in order to share their commitments and values on climate change. From hosting worship for interested delegates to engaging the issues theologically, these faith-based advocates make a difference.

How To's

 Learn what national policies exist regarding climate change, fuel efficiency for vehicles, industry emission caps, and air pollution. The strength of environmental laws has a tremendous impact on efforts to care for God's creation. Find policy updates and/or action alerts from your denominational public policy offices, ecumenical agencies, state council of churches, the National Council of Churches, and other organizations you trust.

 Know your legislators—both nationally and locally—and tell them what you think. Find out who represents you locally, at the state level, and in Congress at http://www.usa.gov/Contact/Elected.shtml.

 Share your views through your local newspaper or radio station.

Learn, and celebrate, the steps toward energy efficiency that have been taken in your congregation, school district, and region.

Demand investigation of industry practices by local government and organize for fair citizen oversight if industries seem to be violating the law.

FAITH MATTERS

What does the Holy One require of you but to do justice, and to love kindness, and to walk humbly with your God?

MICAH 6:8

ENERGY

Most of us get some of the energy we use on a daily basis from coal. Coal mining has long been part of energy production in the United States, but a new way of harvesting coal began in the 1970s called mountaintop removal. This method of removing coal uses fewer people and more machines as it blows up mountains and fills in valleys. The people in Appalachia suffer effects from loss of mining jobs, declining property values, battles over land rights, air pollution, pollution of their drinking water, and the destruction of their home landscape. Some people are even dying because of the pollution created by this type of mining. The natural systems in Appalachia also suffer from air and water pollution, clear cutting, flooding, destruction of habitat, soil erosion, and more. While this method of mining may be more cost-effective for industries, it helps neither the local economy nor the environment. It is destroying the country's oldest mountains as well as threatening a distinct culture.

How To's

1 **Learn how much of your energy comes from coal, and where that coal comes from.** Your local gas and electric companies should be able to answer these questions. Also, the organization I Love Mountains has a "Show My Connection to MTR" tool with a map feature at http://www.ilovemountains.org.

2 **Take a mission trip to Appalachia** to hear from the people and congregations who live in the midst of these mining operations.

3 **Advocate for public policies** that will stop the destruction of mountains and culture in Appalachia.

4 **Support organizations that are actively supporting the end of mountaintop removal,** such as I Love Mountains.

5 **Organize a group** in your neighborhood or church to watch *Kilowatt Ours* or another film that shows what mountaintop removal looks like.

Walking the Talk

In West Virginia, Allen Johnson started an organization called Christians for the Mountains whose mission is to recognize our responsibility to live compatibly and sustainably upon God's earth. Johnson says that his environmental advocacy stems from his deep hope and faith in God's inbreaking kingdom. While Johnson has experience in both charismatic churches and Brethren congregations, this organization brings together Christians of all affiliations. Through education, advocacy, and prayer, Christians for the Mountains seeks to end mountaintop removal extraction. Its members are joined by concerned Christians in Appalachia and across the nation to educate people about mountaintop removal and to advocate the cessation of the practice.

FAITH MATTERS

They put their hand to the flinty rock, and overturn mountains by the roots. They cut out channels in the rocks, and their eyes see every precious thing. The sources of the rivers they probe; hidden things they bring to light. But where shall wisdom be found? And where is the place of understanding?

JOB 28:9–12

ENERGY

The energy used, the pollution produced, and the resources consumed by buildings have significant impact on climate change. The health of people (particularly vulnerable populations such as children, the elderly, and people with limited income) as well as the health of the environment are affected by the way we build. There exist logical, natural, and healthy ways to build and to renovate that are attentive to the health of people and the planet.

How To's

1 **Consult local green architects and resources** for help with green building and renovating. The U.S. Green Building Council (http://www.usgbc.org) has many resources, including LEED standards and renovation suggestions. (Choose the top LEED standards in order to be truly eco-friendly.) The Eco-Justice Working Group of the National Council of Churches has a green building guide for congregations (http://www.nccecojustice.org). Consult the American Institute of Architects to find architects who specialize in green building.

2 **Choose the best site** if you are building new. Consider accessibility by foot, bicycle, and mass transit. Consider natural shade, thermal mass, and drainage as you choose your site.

3 **Incorporate green elements at the design stage.** These elements include energy efficiency, water conservation, renewable energy usage, and nontoxic building materials.

4 **Enough is better than more.** The smaller the building, the less energy needed for heating, cooling, and lighting.

5 **Insulate.** Install good insulation in your walls and reflective panels in your attic. Buy doors and windows that keep a tight seal. Most hardware stores will be able to give you good energy-saving advice.

6 **Use the right materials.** Find building materials that can be reused from older buildings such as old kitchen tile. Choose materials that have a reduced environmental footprint, such as bamboo, reclaimed wood, or certified sustainable wood from the Forestry Stewardship Council. Linoleum is more natural and less toxic than vinyl. Find out which carpet and tile companies take back the product at the end of its life. Use local materials to save the energy-intensive aspect of transporting products from other areas of the world. Avoid products with formaldehyde. Paint with low-VOC (volatile organic compound) paint.

Walking the Talk

Members of St. Andrew Christian Church in Olathe, Kansas, decided to include natural building methods in a renovation of their church. They used straw bale walls for the entrance room before the sanctuary. These walls remind them of their sister relationship with a community in El Salvador, where people often build their homes naturally (with adobe). Also, the building process was able to incorporate church members' artistic abilities and sweat equity, so the congregation feels a special connection to, and ownership of, the church building. Finally, the straw bale encourages congregants to remember God's call to care for creation each time they walk through the doors.

Profile online at National Religious Partnership for the Environment, http://www.nrpe.org/profiles/profiles_vi_C_18_01.htm.

7 **Install energy-efficient appliances.** Front-load washers and energy-efficient dishwashers, ovens, and refrigerators will go a long way toward reducing the building's energy use. Do not put the oven and refrigerator next to each other.

8 **Go low-flow or no-flow.** Installing low-flow toilets and faucets and no-flow urinals early in the building process will ensure the long-term reduction of water use as well as a reduction in the energy used to heat water.

9 **When possible, build with what nature provides!** Check your local building codes and find ways to incorporate cob, straw bale, and rammed earth in your building projects. These alternative, creative, and fun building materials will enliven any project, and they save money as well. One Web site that covers a variety of natural building techniques and resources is http://www.greenhomebuilding.com/natural_building.htm.

FAITH MATTERS

Ah, you who join house to house, who add field to field, until there is room for no one but you, and you are left to live alone in the midst of the land!

ISAIAH 5:8

ENERGY

Most energy audits will include recommendations that are simple, economical changes as well as some longer-term, more expensive suggestions. A complete energy audit of your property is the surest way to know that the changes you are making are having the impact you want.

How To's

1 **Research who in your area does audits** and how much they cost. Some gas and electric service providers and nonprofits will do audits for low or no cost.

2 **Ask the auditor if you can be a part of the audit.** You do not want to interfere with the audit itself, but you could learn a great deal.

3 **Decide which recommendations you can pursue** easily and which will take more work.

4 As you apply recommendations, **be sure your family or congregation knows what you are doing and why.** While any action is effective in and of itself, it is always more effective if as many people as possible know the action is happening. Your action can have ripple effects as new people learn about your commitment, values, and new experience.

5 **Don't forget to celebrate!** Once you've taken steps to reduce your home energy use, track the changes on your energy bill. Hang those reduced bills on the fridge or bulletin board!

Walking the Talk

Andrew Rudin, project coordinator of New Jersey's Interfaith Coalition on Energy, audited First Presbyterian Church in Pitman, New Jersey. The church implemented many energy-saving measures and found them worthwhile, both economically and environmentally. The church upgraded the furnace, replaced windows, upgraded lighting with energy-efficient technology (including exit signs), and added thermostats to many rooms to increase savings when not in use.

As with all areas of action and advocacy, there comes a time to realize that inaction may also be one's call. Sometimes it is useful to engage in activities that neither produce nor pollute. As we delve into energy concerns, how might we enjoy our own energies, and those of all creation, as we attend to the goodness, glory, and graciousness of our Creator?

How To's

1 **Unplug computers, televisions, and other electronic gadgets** and revel instead in storytelling, conversation, playing games, sharing meals, and other ways of enjoying life without using fossil fuel energy.

2 **Unwind.** Decide not to drive anywhere today nor to turn on the oven. Curl up with a good book under a tree instead.

3 **Take a walk outside,** away from air conditioning or heating.

4 **Create art!** Sculpt, draw, collage, or paint as a way to respond to the Creator of the universe.

5 **Go on a picnic** to enjoy the fruits of the earth and the companionship of the world around you.

Walking the Talk

Earth Hour, an event organized by the World Wildlife Fund, was held in Sydney, Australia, in 2007 and around the world in 2008. It involved turning off lights for one hour in order to demonstrate commitment to curbing climate change. Churches and theological institutions as well as homes, city buildings, and businesses were all encouraged to participate. In Mississauga, Ontario, members of the Christian Reformed Church of Meadowvale met in their sanctuary to worship with the lights off and with a small, contained fire burning. They read Scripture (by memory or by the light of candles or flashlights), they sang, and they danced in this unique worship service connected to Earth Hour.

Sophie Vandenberg, "Ontario Church Observes Earth Hour," *The Banner*, June 2008, http://www.thebanner.org/magazine/article.cfm?article_id=1562.

FAITH MATTERS

God will guide you continually, and satisfy your needs in parched places, and make your bones strong; and you shall be like a watered garden, like a spring of water, whose waters never fail.
ISAIAH 58:11

2. FOOD AND

The pesticides, monocropping, and fossil-fueled technology used by industrial agriculture require immense water and energy resources. Subsequently, the transportation of food from the field to the store, and from the store to our table, burns even more fossil fuels. In these ways, our food choices intimately impact climate change.

The circle continues as the floods and droughts of climate change—phenomena at least partly brought about by the use of fossil fuels in modern industrial agriculture—mean unpredictable and harsher circumstances for farmers around the world, as well as food shortages for those who depend on food brought from long distances.

AGRICULTURE

Much of the fossil fuel energy used to produce food is consumed through the transportation of food from far distances. Did you know that food travels, on average, more than 1,500 miles to your table? Energy is also consumed in large-scale industrial agriculture by the heavy use of pesticides and the fuel for farm equipment. Eating locally and seasonally supports the local economy and ensures the livelihood of local family farmers—who usually have smaller farms, who are more responsible caregivers of the land, and who are a vital part of a healthy local economy.

Supporting local or regional farmers in your community, and encouraging the self-reliance of small farmers around the world, helps local communities to have "food sovereignty." Food sovereignty means that no international trade policies nor any global food crisis will make any one particular community extremely vulnerable to hunger.

How To's

1 **Find out where and when your town has farmers' markets or farm stands** and support them! Search http://www.localharvest.org to find the ones closest to where you live.

2 **Talk to local farmers.** Ask what led them into farming, what their farms are like, and what farming methods they use to treat pests and weeds. Knowing this information can help you make decisions as to what to buy.

3 **Find out if any local farms sponsor a Community Supported Agriculture (CSA) program.** In a CSA, you pledge an advance commitment to buy direct from that particular farm during its growing season. In return, you are ensured a regular supply of fresh produce and the farm is ensured a predictable and sustainable customer. CSAs create a special relationship between farmer and customer, and most CSAs are open to your visiting the farm to become even more familiar with the food you eat. Search http://www.localharvest.org to find a CSA near you.

4 **Ask your grocery stores when and where they stock local produce.** If they do not, ask them why they do not and if they would consider it in the future.

Walking the Talk

In 2000, Rev. John Pitney, a United Methodist pastor in Eugene, Oregon, started the "That's My Farmer" project, which provides church-based support for local farmers. This growing project supports twelve different farms through nearly twenty faith communities. At First United Methodist Church, where Pitney is associate pastor, fifty families support local farms through CSA shares. Another two hundred people from other faith communities in the area also participate, bringing the total contributions to farmers to approximately $50,000 a year. Every spring, First Church hosts a festival at which people and farmers get to meet each other and farmers have the chance to share their stories and faith journeys. This effort has had wide-ranging impact, from teaching children that vegetables grow in a season (and taste best when just picked) to encouraging adults to think about how their consumer commitments reflect their theological values. Meanwhile, local farmers truly feel the financial, social, and prayer support of the faith community as they produce healthy food and strengthen the local economy.

http://www.diocese-oregon.org/artman/publish/printer_481.shtml, http://www.umtv.org/archives/thats_my_farmer.htm, and http://gbgm-umc.org/global_news/full_article.cfm?articleid=4336

5 **Eat at restaurants that cook with local ingredients.** For instance, the Northwest chain Burgerville is a sustainable business that uses seasonal produce (huckleberry milkshakes and Walla Walla onion rings) and purchases local beef from a rancher cooperative in Oregon. These commitments go hand in hand with the company's purchase of 100 percent wind energy and its transformation of used cooking grease into biodiesel.[1]

FAITH MATTERS

These all look to you to give them their food in due season; when you give to them, they gather it up; when you open your hand, they are filled with good things.

PSALM 104:27–28

FOOD AND AGRIGCULTURE

Because organic means no toxic pesticides are used (which are energy intensive in their production), eating organic is one step on the way to curbing climate change. Many nonorganic foods now contain added hormones, artificial ingredients, pesticides, and genetically engineered ingredients, all of which have negative environmental impacts.

While eating organic products and sustainably raised meats and dairy is usually better for the environment, plants, and animals, it is helpful to keep step one (eating local) in mind. If the choice is between an organic item from a huge food conglomerate that has just recently jumped onto the organic bandwagon and ships its products from across the country, it is probably better to buy food locally from farmers you know and trust. Organic produce from thousands of miles away still burns fossil fuels in the transportation process.

How To's

1 Ask at farm stands and farmers' markets which produce and meats are organic or sustainably raised. While some small farmers cannot afford either the time or money involved in becoming "certified" organic (and some may refuse because of the recent industry involvement in USDA organic standards), most producers will tell you what methods they use to keep pests and weeds away.

2 If your local grocery doesn't have an organic section, ask if the store has individual organic items. If it has neither a dedicated section nor any organic items, ask the manager to start carrying some basic organic items (even better if they are local!)

3 When you are choosing between organic foods, buy foods that are in season and that are as close to your geographic location as possible.

4 Find the "Shoppers' Guide to Pesticides in Produce" list and take it to the grocery store with you (http://www.foodnews.org). Developed by analysts from the Environmental Working Group, this guide gives you the scoop on what they call the "dirty dozen" and the "cleanest twelve"—which foods you should definitely buy organic and which nonorganic foods are okay if organics are not available.

Walking the Talk

Audrey Wilkinson and her husband Steve, both members of the Christian Reformed Church of Canada, started buying organics a few years ago after a health condition arose and Audrey read how much better organic eating could be for her. She reflects, "The more I researched the topic, the more I felt convicted that buying organic and locally grown items is a much bigger issue than just me being healthier. I love food and have always seen my calling as one that involved food, so when I felt God nudging me to dig deeper, I did. I found that buying and eating organic and locally grown food is a matter of stewardship as much as it is about social justice and what God calls us all to do and be. By utilizing these resources we do not only help our bodies stay healthy, but we also cause less harm to the earth and animals that have been given into our care (Gen 1:29–30)."

FAITH MATTERS

You cause the grass to grow for the cattle, and plants for people to use, to bring forth food from the earth, and wine to gladden the human heart, oil to make the face shine, and bread to strengthen the human heart.

PSALM 104:14–15

FOOD AND AGRIGCULTURE

The production of meat is a highly energy-intensive process. The amount of food, water, and habitat needed per animal, as well as the energy to maintain the industry, all contribute to the burning of fossil fuels. The Intergovernmental Panel on Climate Change (IPCC) 2007 report received worldwide attention and won the group the Nobel Peace Prize.[2] The report encouraged lifestyle changes to reduce each person's contribution to climate change. The head of the IPCC, Rajendra Pachauri, named eating less meat as one crucial way people can lessen their carbon footprint.[3]

Did you know?

Producing one kilo (2.2 pounds) of beef, lamb, or pork causes the emissions equivalent of 36.4 kilos of carbon dioxide. Raising and transporting that two pounds of meat requires the same amount of energy as lighting a 100-watt bulb for nearly three weeks. ("Lifestyle Changes Can Curb Climate Change: IPCC Chief," Agence France-Presse, January 15, 2008, http://afp.google.com/article/ALeqM5iIVBkZpOUA9Hz3Xc2u-61mDlrw0Q.)

In the fall of 2006, the United Nations Food and Agriculture Organization reported that the meat industry contributes more greenhouse gas emissions than all forms of transportation combined. (Claudia H. Deutsch, "Trying to Connect the Dinner Plate to Climate Change," August 29, 2007, http://www.nytimes.com/2007/08/29/business/media/29adco.html)

While livestock industries contribute to climate change, they also contribute to pollution. Factory farms produce about 500 million tons of waste—three times the waste of the national human population. Farm waste leads to air, water, and soil pollution. (Humane Society of the United States, "This Earth Day, Eat Cool Foods to Fight Global Warming," April 21, 2008, http://www.hsus.org/farm/news/ournews/this_earth_day_eat_cool_foods.html)

Cows constantly produce methane, the second most significant greenhouse gas. The more cows, the more methane. ("Fifty Things to Do to Stop Global Warming," http://globalwarming-facts.info/50-tips.html)

Walking the Talk

The Christian Vegetarian Association, an international, nondenominational organization, encourages plant-based nutrition. The pastors, doctors, and educators on its board and in its membership profess that a vegetarian diet is a faithful and healthy lifestyle for Christians and that such a diet benefits people, animals, and the environment. The organization explains, "Our bodies are ill-suited to manage the huge quantities of meat that many people consume, such as three servings a day, and modern animal agriculture produces particularly unhealthy foods."

How To's

1. **Reduce your meat intake.** Set concrete goals and create an evaluation process to check your progress.

2. **Find family, congregational, or community support** to reduce meat and to enjoy meat-free dining together.

3. **Find vegetarian ingredients and foods** to substitute in some of your favorite meals.

4. **Shop farmers' markets for meat** that hasn't been transported cross-country or raised in an overly energy-consumptive atmosphere.

FAITH MATTERS

God said, "See, I have given you every plant yielding seed that is upon the face of all the earth, and every tree with seed in its fruit; you shall have them for food. And to every beast of the earth, and to every bird of the air, and to everything that creeps on the earth, everything that has the breath of life, I have given every green plant for food."

GENESIS 1:29–30

FOOD AND AGRICULTURE

While supporting local farmers, eating organic, and eating lower on the food chain are all healthy and helpful, gardening is the hands-on way to connect with the beautiful biodiversity of God's good earth. It is the most direct way to make sure food, seeds, and the knowledge of growing food stays in the local community. It is also a way to make sure heirloom plants do not become extinct and that your produce is raised exactly with your standards. When it comes to climate change, small gardens with a variety of plantings may be a good way for local communities to prepare for the droughts and floods that may continue to increase as well as a good way to fight the possible food shortages related thereto. Finally, gardening is a fun way to teach children empathy for the earth and their responsibility to care for it.

How To's

1 Patronize local nurseries and garden stores.

2 Look for seeds and seedlings that have not been genetically modified. For the most part, certified organic seeds should not be genetically modified. Also, you can collect your own seeds from any plants that have bolted at the end of the season or exchange seeds with other gardeners.

3 Choose heirloom varieties of plants in order to keep biodiversity going for future generations.

4 Garden organically, managing insects and weeds without pesticides. Search for organic gardening tips on the Internet, or ask at your local garden store.

5 Search the Internet or ask around to find "master gardeners" or "master composters" in your community and find out if they are willing to help get you started or point you to the best local resources.

6 Work with others if you are able. Community gardens enable people to share expertise, try different plants, exchange produce, and look after one another's plots when needed.

7 Make or buy rain barrels to collect water for your garden from your roof. The energy used to transport and treat the water that runs out of your tap for five minutes would power a 60-watt lightbulb for fourteen hours.[4] One Web site that instructs on building and installing a rain barrel is http://www.swfwmd.state.fl.us/conservation/rainbarrel/make-a-rain-barrel.html.

Walking the Talk

Cedar Grove United Methodist Church in Cedar Grove, North Carolina, opened the Anathoth Community Garden on its grounds in 2005 as a way to help bring people together across boundaries of race, socioeconomic class, age, and gardening experience. The cooperative effort required all participants to work in the garden and then for all to share in the organic produce, which created a sense of community and reconciliation.

From the Web site of the NCC's Eco-Justice Program, http://www.nccecojustice.org/faithharveststories.html.

FAITH MATTERS

The Holy God took the human one and put him in the garden of Eden to till it and keep it.

GENESIS 2:15

Connect Daily Bread to Eucharist

Partaking of the elements of bread and wine (or juice) may not often move us to think about physical food as much as they may draw our attention to spiritual food. Yet the sacrament of the Eucharist, or Lord's Supper, can be a helpful way to remember that Jesus used everyday, physical elements to communicate with his disciples. We also pray, as Jesus taught, to "give us this day our daily bread." Our daily bread, and the meals we eat every day, are indeed a blessing from God, and we should see them as evidence of God's care for us.

Connecting our common act of eating to Eucharist may help us remember how sacred life is.

If we remember in our corporate worship life, and even in our sacraments, that we touch—and are touched by—the earthy elements of God's creation, then our reverence and respect may grow to transform the way we live. This transformation can have a profound impact, including an impact on climate change.

How To's

1 **Provide homemade, local, and/or organic bread and wine or juice** to use for the Eucharist.

2 **Include in the eucharistic prayer mention of God's creation** and the ways we experience God through the glories of what the earth has produced.

3 **Say grace before meals,** recognizing that bread, juice, and all we eat is a gift from God.

4 **Regularly purchase the kind of food that you would be delighted to bring before God** as an offering.

Walking the Talk

Through journaling, art, or conversation with others, reflect on your experience of the Eucharist and how it is connected to your daily food.

Does it change your view of daily food to see it as sacred—as a gift from God?

Does it change your view of the Eucharist to see it as food—as elements of the earth that are full of life, elements that absorbed sun and water and were touched by insects and human hands?

How might the Eucharist transform your worship and, eventually, your life?

What is daily bread? How much nourishment do we need each day, and from what type of food? What happens when we have too little or too much?

FAITH MATTERS

And he said to them, "When you pray, say: Father, hallowed be your name. Your kingdom come. Give us each day our daily bread. And forgive us our sins, for we ourselves forgive everyone indebted to us. And do not bring us to the time of trial."

LUKE 11:2–4

Advocate Sustainable Agricultural Policies

Fair food, sustainable agriculture, and just farming need public policy backing as much if not more than consumer support. Without rules and regulations, we will continue to see huge tracts of monocropped land that is used by industrial agriculture for profit and for export. Family farmers will continue to have to find work off the farm, and the small, complex farms that are the backbone of local food security will continue to diminish. We need to fight for strong policies that are fair to local farmers and that promote sustainable agriculture. Local farmers and sustainable agriculture use energy more efficiently and care for creation better than any large-scale industrial agriculture operation is able to do. As climate change conditions worsen current food crises, families must be able to provide for their own food. Public policies must protect food sovereignty for citizens at local, national, and global levels.

How To's

1 **Research city, state, and federal policies.** How do they support local family farmers, subsidize crops, or zone land for development? Do local farmers receive incentives or penalties for keeping their produce or meats in the local economy rather than exporting them?

2 **Find out from local farmers** at farm stands or farmers' markets what some of the biggest problems are that they face from current public policies.

3 **Advocate for nutritious foods to be accessible to all people.** Poverty and hunger can exist both in urban areas (often because of few or no good grocery stores) and in rural areas (which are surrounded by farms but populated often by people with little expendable income).

4 **Encourage your public school system to get rid of vending machines** and to make school lunch a healthier and more sustainable option for children. To read more and find organizations working on this project, go to http://www.sustainabletable.org/features/articles/backtoschool. Connecting local farms to local schools is a particularly helpful way to advocate for local food economy. On this topic, go to http://www.foodsecurity.org/farm_to_school.html.

5 **Host an adult study in your congregation** of your denomination's policies on food and agriculture.

Walking the Talk

The National Catholic Rural Life Conference has long been a model of advocacy and education work to shape better agricultural policies and help rural people improve the quality of life in their communities (http://www.ncrlc.com). This organization offers insightful commentary on a wide variety of public policy issues related to agriculture as a way of assisting people of faith who want to advocate for better public policies and to help build stronger rural communities.

FAITH MATTERS

The seed shrivels under the clods, the storehouses are desolate; the granaries are ruined because the grain has failed. How the animals groan! The herds of cattle wander about because there is no pasture for them; even the flocks of sheep are dazed.

JOEL 1:17–18

FOOD AND AGRIGCULTURE

Savoring good, fresh, and healthy food in community is a way to celebrate God's creation. It is also a way to become renewed and refreshed in order to continue our commitments and efforts to curb climate change. "Slow Food" is the name of an international movement that arose in response to the great preponderance of fast-food joints (http://www.slowfood.com). Standing in stark contrast to cheap, quickly made, and overly standardized foods consumed by individuals in a rush to get through meals and on with life, Slow Food encourages people to reclaim the pleasure of dining, of taste, of local foods, and of good company. This idea of slowing down as we engage in reclaiming the pleasure of time spent with other people—gathering and cooking with local ingredients, smelling and tasting lovingly prepared food, and enjoying one another—has much to teach us.

How To's

1 **Find recipes that use local, seasonal ingredients** and incorporate them in your cooking.

2 **Use the time right before the meal to say grace**—to be mindful, thankful, and delighted in the gift of food.

3 **Make your meals your evening entertainment.** Instead of wolfing down dinner in order to get to the movies, enjoy a luxurious dinner and good conversation for your entertainment.

4 **Invite friends over for a "slow food" evening** in which you cook and eat together and enjoy one another without rushing to other engagements.

5 On a regular basis with some friends, **share a meal and then engage in a spiritual practice together,** such as contemplative prayer.

Walking the Talk

A small group of friends—including teachers, writers, pastors, and community leaders—gathered one evening in northern California to share a slow evening of food and conversation. They turned off cell phones and other electronic devices and placed them in a basket with their watches for the evening. The evening's activity was cooking, tasting, smelling, laughing, talking, praying, and enjoying. Time, if tracked at all, was only tracked on the kitchen timer needed for cooking. This slow evening was a blessing and a Sabbath for each member of the group, rejuvenating and revitalizing them in an otherwise fast-paced, time-centered world.

FAITH MATTERS

Remove far from me falsehood and lying; give me neither poverty nor riches; feed me with the food that I need, or I shall be full, and deny you, and say, "Who is God?" or I shall be poor, and steal, and profane the name of my God.

PROVERBS 30:8–9

3. TRANSPO

One of the three most influential environmental choices you make as an individual is your mode of transportation.[1] Lessening our dependence on fossil fuel transportation is critical to curbing climate change. We should make choices, when we are able, that are good for our own health and the health of the world. When we expend more of our personal energy in order to move ourselves around, we drastically reduce our need for fossil fuel energy and improve our own mental and physical health.

Don't Be Baffled by Biofuels

O ther than fossil fuel combustion, how can we fuel our demands for energy? First, and most importantly, we must change our sense of entitlement and our ongoing demand for cheap, endless energy. The earth was not created to be consumed greedily by a spiraling human population and its ever-growing demands on natural resources. There is no way around our need to reduce our demand on energy. Second, we must learn about the options and all the implications involved, being careful to hear more than the industry lines on what is available or practical. Finally, we must make choices the best we can, humbly admitting that we always are choosing between imperfect solutions but trying our best to choose the most sustainable options.

What Are Biofuels?

Biofuels cover a broad range of nonpetroleum-based fuels. Biofuels include everything from fuels made from industrial agriculture products (such as corn or sugarcane) to fuels of used vegetable oil—basically any energy source derived from biological matter. We must ask questions about where natural resources are used in the manufacturing process, about the waste created by the process, and about how the fuels will affect the market related to the source product. If deforestation or overconsumption of local water sources is necessary to plant crops that will then be harvested and processed for fuel, is that fuel truly sustainable? If we are producing large tracts of plants to feed our oil addiction while people starve around the world, is it really an eco-justice solution? We must pursue non–fossil fuel energy, but we also must be cautious and thoughtful about appropriate alternatives.

How To's

1 Research differences between various types of biofuels, particularly corn ethanol, cellulosic ethanol, and biodiesel (the most popular categories in the overall debate).[2]

2 Ask questions, such as: What are the impacts of the pesticides and fertilizers used to raise the crops that will be converted to fuel? How much energy does the manufacturing process use? What greenhouse gases does the process produce? What percentage of the total crop gets converted to energy? How much land will be used? Could those crops or the land be better used by local communities to feed themselves? Who benefits most from biofuels? To read more from those concerned

Walking the Talk

In 2006, Rick Ufford-Chase, a former Moderator of the Presbyterian Church (U.S.A.) General Assembly and current director of Presbyterian Peace Fellowship, and his family decided to try driving on used vegetable oil as one way to live faithfully with God's creation. They bought a used Volkswagen with a conversion kit for allowing it to run on vegetable oil for fuel (once the car had warmed up). Cars such as that driven by the Ufford-Chase family often have exhaust fumes that smell like fast-food restaurant fries because, in fact, the fuel had originally been used to cook such fried foods!

http://www.pcusa.org/today/cover/2007/cover0507.htm

with agricultural products being used for fuel, go to the Family Farm Defenders' Agrofuels Campaign at http://www.familyfarmdefenders.org/pmwiki.php/Agrofuels/Agrofuels.

3 **Be wary of any trumpeted "ideal" solution** that makes increased profits for industrial agriculture, oil companies, or governments without drastically reducing greenhouse gases, tightening fuel-efficiency standards, and providing access to all people.

4 **Do not be tempted to think any one option can substitute for our current overconsumption of fuel.** We will most likely need a variety of solutions, including local options created by small cooperatives (such as local biodiesel plants). We need to fight for continued policies of fuel efficiency and the conversion of engines for clean burning of whatever fuel is used. Finally, there is no way around the bottom line—the drastic reduction of daily habits of energy consumption.

FAITH MATTERS

God, you created the world and called it good. Yet we consume natural resources at a frightening pace to fuel our fast-paced lives. As we enter a period of food crises, climate change, and increased population, guide us in your wisdom to find ways to limit our energy use and to find sustainable energy sources.

The development of sustainable fuels is needed. However, no matter what kind of fuel we use, if the vehicle into which we pour it is not fuel efficient, we have only solved a small part of the problem. In the United States, people like cars—and that means sedans, minivans, trucks, and SUVs. People choose vehicles for a variety of reasons, including cost, comfort, popularity, brand loyalty, design, and marketing. As the price of gasoline fluctuates, another factor in decision making is fuel efficiency. In 2008, for the first time in a long time, small cars became popular again. People now know that big cars have big gas tanks, which can mean spending big dollars, not to mention making a big impact on climate change.

How To's

1 **In general, choose small.** The larger the vehicle, the fewer miles per gallon. The same goes for heavier vehicles and vehicles that are not aerodynamic (roof racks, for instance, add a lot of drag).

2 **Drive smart.** Avoid quick acceleration and high speeds (studies have shown that 55 miles per hour is one of the best speeds for fuel efficiency). More driving tips are available at http://www.greenercars.org/drivingtips.htm.

3 **Maintain your vehicle.** Keep the tires inflated, the car empty of extra weight, and the exterior clean.

4 When shopping for a new vehicle, **choose the most energy-efficient model you can afford.** The EPA has an online rating system for cars at http://www.epa.gov/greenvehicles. You can also compare cars at http://www.greenercars.org or http://www.fueleconomy.gov.

5 **Let companies know you are assessing their products** and be honest about your expectations and demands. Fuel efficiency is something that car manufacturers can build into vehicles.

6 **Advocate for better funding for research** on electric cars, plug-in hybrids, fuel cell cars, and other fuel-efficient technologies.

Walking the Talk

In 2002 Rev. Denny Hook and his wife Barbara purchased their first Toyota Prius, a hybrid vehicle. They were so pleased with it that they purchased another Prius a few years later. They bought these cars in order to save carbon dioxide emissions, believing that everything we do makes a difference to the earth. Hook comments, "At one point in my life I saw myself as a United Methodist minister with a passion for the environment. Now I see myself as a passionate lover of the earth who just happens to be a UM minister." His commitments have shaped his theology. He explains, "Salvation no longer means our species going to heaven but salvation means restoring the balance of the earth." By driving their hybrid vehicles, the Hooks are trying to help restore that balance.

FAITH MATTERS

Holy God, we are thankful for the ease and freedom that automobiles bring into our lives. Yet we are aware how easy it is to become too dependent on them and to forget that our choices may limit someone else's ease and freedom in another part of the world or in another generation. Help us to make good choices now so that the emissions from our vehicles and the culture of consumerism do not harm another part of your creation.

In big cities, residents often use public transit as a habit; driving and parking are actually much more troublesome than using public transportation. In smaller cities and towns, public transportation may be available but inconvenient or restrictive. And in some towns and rural areas, public transportation may not be a part of the regional infrastructure at all. However, we all can participate in some type of public transit in some way—indeed, it is vital to support the idea, and the reality, of public transportation. It is a much more economical and environmental alternative to individual fossil-fueled vehicles.

How To's

1 **Learn what options your community has:** metro, light rail, subway, city buses, shared shuttle vans.

2 For out-of-state travel, **know where your closest train and bus stations are,** as well as what the prices and schedules are.

3 **Set aside an afternoon or day for a local "transportation treasure hunt"** using public transit. Include your church youth groups, children's groups, or family members. Plan a route that will bring you to a fun destination or two (e.g., ice cream parlor, coffee shop, museum, or sporting event) and to a practical destination or two (e.g., grocery store, pharmacy, department store). Make sure everyone knows the basic schedules and timetables and has the fare needed for the rides.

4 If you do not have access to public transportation, **ask town or city officials why this is so.** Encourage them to consider some way to alleviate the situation where everyone must depend on individual automobiles.

5 If you do have a fairly decent system, **pledge to support it on a regular basis** that makes sense for you. Set goals and meet them. Evaluate after a few weeks what it is like to use public transportation. Write a letter to the editor or to the city or town council to express your views.

Walking the Talk

Susan Ellison, former PCUSA mission worker in Bolivia, is now pursuing a PhD in anthropology at Brown University, where she can transport herself by foot or public transportation to school as well as to the grocery store. When she travels to church on Sunday, she generally walks two miles to take a bus to Boston, switches lines twice, and walks a few more blocks. This two-hour, one-way trip allows Susan to read, appreciate the scenery, and enjoy some quiet time for reflection. Susan intentionally decided not to own a car in order to cut back on her oil dependency, both for environmental reasons and for geopolitical reasons. Having lived overseas and seen the effects of U.S. consumption in other communities around the world, Susan believes that our choices make a difference. She explains, "I feel committed to the community and to using public transportation. When people use public transportation, it becomes important to and valued by the community and will then be better maintained by the city." In inclement weather, Susan will try to carpool to church or may even decide to stay home, recognizing that staying home on occasion is one acceptable side effect of not owning a car.

6 If you use public transportation but your friends and family do not, **plan activities together in which you take them on a bus or a train.** Also, mention interesting stories of your experiences in casual conversation in order to normalize the experience of riding public transit.

FAITH MATTERS

Now the whole group of those who believed were of one heart and soul, and no one claimed private ownership of any possessions, but everything they owned was held in common.

ACTS 4:32

Check Out Carpooling and Ridesharing

The *Blondie* comic strip every so often will show Dagwood either rushing out the door to meet his car pool, or in the car with three other people on their way to work. Yet carpooling seems less prevalent than it used to be. With busier lives, more individualized work schedules, and multiple destinations often planned for one trip, people tend to resort to driving their own vehicle for independence and convenience. However, with unpredictable gas prices and the reality of climate change, we might find that a little short-term inconvenience now will go a long way to alleviating the long-term "inconvenience" caused by the natural disasters, food shortages, and other predicted outcomes of climate change.

How To's

 Draw up a schedule of your regular activities—work, school, and leisure—particularly those you do on a fairly predictable basis, either daily, weekly, or monthly. Consider if anyone who lives nearby also participates in any of those activities. Propose trying to carpool a few times to see how it works for all parties.

 Draw up a schedule of regular errands, particularly those you do on an "as needed" basis. Think of others who shop at the same places as you shop who might be willing to make at least a few "errand dates" with you. It will give you time to visit, help one another out, and lessen your greenhouse gas emissions.

 Share the driving and/or the cost of gas in order to maintain good relations within the car pool.

 Be on time to show your respect for one another's time commitments.

For more carpool tips, **see http://www.erideshare.com/ information**.htm.

If you are interested in finding a rideshare, **contact the numbers often listed on local road signs, call your local government office, or check out an online rideshare Web site** such as http://www.erideshare.com. Do not travel with someone you do not trust.

Walking the Talk

While rushing out the door to church and driving quickly to avoid being late to worship, have you ever wondered about this ironic lack of community—and lack of time to notice or appreciate God's creation—that precipitates the gathering in the pews? The Environmental Committee at All Souls Church in Washington, D.C., decided in 2007 that one of its priorities was to develop a rideshare program. The committee created a sign-up board for members to connect with one another and publicized the program on Earth Day 2008. Ridesharing to church is a great way to have a few extra moments of conversation and community before and after weekly worship, as well as a way to curb carbon emissions.

To read more about this church and its environmental commitments, visit its Web site at http://www.all-souls.org.

FAITH MATTERS

Two are better than one, because they have a good reward for their toil. For if they fall, one will lift up the other; but woe to one who is alone and falls and does not have another to help.

ECCLESIASTES 4:9–10

So what do we do when it's time for a long-distance work trip or vacation? If a car, bus, or train isn't going to take you to your destination, how do airplanes or cruise ships compare as travel options? For most people, it will not come as a surprise to learn that air travel has much worse greenhouse gas emissions than driving or taking a bus or train, no matter what the distance. Meanwhile, traveling by sea also has some serious environmental implications. While ocean liners and cruise ships may be a fun way to travel on the deep blue sea, there are no regulations of any kind on their greenhouse gas emissions.

Air Travel Facts of Interest

Air travel accounts for 4–9 percent of all greenhouse gas emissions.

Emissions from airplanes include carbon dioxide, nitrous oxide, sulphate, and soot.

Because airplanes cruise at high altitude, their impact on climate change is estimated to be two to four times greater than their greenhouse gas emissions. In other words, the emissions created at a high altitude have more immediate atmospheric and chemical reactions.

The feathery trails left behind by airplanes, called contrails, actually trap heat and lead to global warming.

International flights do not come under any particular country's goal to reduce emissions, so for the most part there is no concerted effort to reduce the emissions from these flights.

(From the David Suzuki Foundation at http://www.davidsuzuki.org/
Climate_Change/What_You_Can_Do/air_travel.asp)

Ship Travel Facts of Interest

No international treaty, not even the Kyoto Protocol, has limited emissions from ocean travel.

Greenhouse gas emissions from ships include carbon dioxide, nitrous oxide, and black carbon (soot). Black carbon warms the air hundreds of thousands of times more than carbon dioxide.

The global marine fleet annually emits approximately the same greenhouse gases as 130 million cars, about the number of cars in the United States. A single ship can emit more greenhouse gases than two thousand diesel trucks.

Emissions from ships are anticipated to triple 2002 levels by 2030.

(From Oceana at http://www.oceana.org/climate/solutions/oceana/no-more-free-ride)

Walking the Talk

In April 2007, United Methodists worldwide were invited to a meeting to hear from denominational leaders about their denomination's membership, ministries, missions, and visioning. Unlike most denominational gatherings, however, this one occurred by teleconference. This "town hall" meeting, as it was considered, included 200 callers (some of whom were a group of people around a single phone, such as small committees at individual churches). Using this new technology enabled the denomination to communicate vital information with members around the world, to answer questions, and to form a sense of community while at the same time not contributing to climate change through participant air travel.

Marta Aldrich, "'Town Hall' Gathering Offers Snapshot of the Church," United Methodist News Service, April 18, 2007, http://www.umc.org/site/apps/nlnet/content2.aspx?c=lwL4KnN1LtH&b=2667549&content_id={02931A64-9E83-43AB-972D-F70E91BD3753}&notoc=1.

How To's

1 **Limit air and ocean travel** by instead using webcam Internet phone calls to connect with friends and family, videoconferencing for work, and vacationing closer to home.

2 When traveling on airplanes, **travel during the day, pack lightly, and purchase carbon offsets.** (More tips are available at http://www.davidsuzuki.org/Climate_Change/What_You_Can_Do/air_travel.asp.)

3 **Contact your legislators** to share your concern about the impact of air and ocean travel, and ask them to pass emissions regulations for these sectors, so that these modes of travel can become cleaner options.

4 **Purchase carbon offsets** when you do need to travel by sea or sky, and look for ways you can otherwise limit long-distance travel.

We consume a lot of fossil fuel energy in order to do things that our own bodies might be able to manage themselves. Expending personal energy is a way to save fossil fuel energy. Walking or bicycling when you are able saves carbon emissions from being produced by your automobile. Also, while obesity and other diseases related to lack of exercise are on the rise in both children and adults, it is ironic that many of us frequently drive distances that are within easy walking or cycling distance. It is as if we are keeping ourselves away from activities that could improve our lives!

Facts from the Union of Concerned Scientists[3]

Motor vehicles are responsible for almost a quarter of annual U.S. emissions of carbon dioxide, the primary global-warming gas.

The U.S. transportation sector alone emits more carbon dioxide than the total emissions in all but three other countries.

Transportation is the largest single source of air pollution in the United States. It caused over half of the carbon monoxide, over a third of the nitrogen oxides, and almost a quarter of the hydrocarbons in our atmosphere in 2006.[4]

How To's

1 For your health and the health of the planet, **walk, bike, and take public transportation** as much as you are able. Set goals and continually evaluate your progress to increase your car independence.

2 Encourage your town or city council to look into making bike lines or taking other steps to improve bike safety, if these steps haven't yet been taken. Also, find out if there is a local cycling club that has done work on these issues and/or would be willing to help.

3 Write editorials or join with others in making a public service announcement on local stations to encourage pedestrian and cycle safety as well as driver respect and attentiveness.

Walking the Talk

Congregations across the nation are realizing how alternate means of arriving to church can be ways to promote community, slow down, and care for creation. For instance, University Baptist Church in Seattle hosted a Drive-Less Sunday for which congregants carpooled, walked, or bicycled to church. The community, collaboration, and creation care involved in such a unique alternate to the average Sunday morning driving rush can serve as a model for countless other congregations.

http://www.earthministry.org/Congregations/stories/CFAC/UBC_On_the_Road.htm

4 When choosing where you live, where you shop, or where you have appointments (such as doctors), **consider how close you will be to where you need to get.** Living within walking, bicycling, or bus-riding distance will increase the chance that you will use these modes of transportation on a regular basis.

5 Host a walk- or bike-to-church Sunday. See "Walking the Talk," and search the Internet for other good stories and ideas.

FAITH MATTERS

I call heaven and earth to witness against you today that
I have set before you life and death, blessings and curses.
Choose life so that you and your descendants may live.

DEUTERONOMY 30:19–20

TRANSPORTATION

Have you ever felt an internal battle between the nagging sensation you should be out running around, "being productive," and your heart's desire to stay at home, read on the couch, work in the garden, or take a stroll through the neighborhood? While it won't do for us to always choose our heart's desire, this one is worth giving in to on occasion. If you need to run out and buy more tissues, can it wait until you also run out of milk? Staying at home and letting your body settle into a slower pace can be a gift, a blessing, and a challenge. It can be a way to claim some Sabbath time from a frenetic pace and to know that one way to conserve energy is to conserve your own energy.

How To's

 Plan days to just be around your home or neighborhood. Your body will thank you for the break from the car!

 See how many days per month you can be on a "car fast," enjoying your time at and around home or using other means of transportation such as bus, bike, or feet.

 Call to find out if a store is open or if it has the product you want rather than driving there to check.

4 **Shop online** for products you would have to drive the farthest to purchase.

5 **Prioritize your time at home,** so that home-based projects, entertainment, meals, and community gatherings become sources of entertainment that are more fun and interesting than those which you would have to cross town to find.

6 **Realize that you are able to get along without most of the things you would be picking up on an errand,** at least for a few days.

Walking the Talk

Peter Sawtell, director of Eco-Justice Ministries, will stay at home if he is invited to fly across the country for only a short engagement. For faraway events, he often asks planners to include enough activities to justify the carbon footprint of the trip. He has also used videoconferencing for a short presentation instead of flying. Peter says, "As I've become more aware of the environmental impact of these trips, I can no longer justify jaunts that don't engage lots of people on the other end." In conjunction with the board of Eco-Justice Ministries, he developed criteria to determine when trips are necessary and helpful and when their benefits don't justify the energy they consume and the pollution they produce.

FAITH MATTERS

This is the Holy One's doing; it is marvelous in our eyes.
This is the day that the Holy One has made; let us rejoice
and be glad in it.

PSALM 118:23–24

4. WATER

When we dam water, the flooded plankton, plant life, and other debris in the reservoir release global warming gases (carbon dioxide and methane) into the atmosphere.[1] Also, in the production of bottled water, huge amounts of fossil fuel energy are used to produce the plastic and then to transport the bottled water around the world. Just as global water processes affect climate change, so climate change affects water. For instance, warming water, melting sea ice, and lack of food affect ocean currents and ocean life. Also, as climate change worsens, so do precipitation patterns, causing increased storms, floods, and droughts. As we change our attitudes and actions in our use of water, so will we lessen our impact on global climate change. In return, this will be good for the waters of the world.

Reduce Personal Water Consumption

WATER

This is not a suggestion to drink less water. It is, instead, a suggestion to curtail wasteful, personal use of water in our homes and congregations. There are both simple and more complicated things that we can do to reduce our water consumption. While one in six people in the world still lacks access to safe drinking water, most of us in the United States have potable water whenever we want.[2] If we had to walk a few miles for the water we use to drink, clean, and cook, we probably would think a bit more about it and would certainly use less of it. While the world's population grows, access to clean water is going to become an increasingly serious concern.

How To's

1 **Purchase a front-loading washing machine.** It uses half the water of a top-loading washer.

2 **Turn off the tap when possible** while washing dishes, brushing teeth, and showering (and take quick showers!).

3 **Save a flush.** One toilet flush in the United States wastes the same amount of water that the average person in a developing nation uses all day for washing, drinking, cooking, and cleaning.[3]

4 **Use low-flow technology.** Replace showerheads and hose nozzles with low-flow models, put a water bottle or other object in the toilet tank to displace a certain amount of water, or buy a low-flow toilet. Some of these methods will reduce water waste by half.

5 **Reuse "gray water."** Keep a bucket in the bath or shower to catch the water wasted while waiting for hot water to arrive. Use this gray water to water your garden or indoor plants or to flush the toilet. Reusing reduces waste 100 percent!

6 When gardening, **conserve water by using drip irrigation** so the water goes directly to the plants' roots. If you can't install drip irrigation, be sure to water in the early morning or late evening to conserve water.

7 **Encourage individuals at your church to reduce water use,** both at church and at home, by hanging signs in kitchens and bathrooms.

Walking the Talk

Aimee Moiso, campus minister for ecumenical and interfaith ministries at Santa Clara University in California, was attending a conference in which attendees were asked at one point to turn to their neighbors and discuss access to clean water in their countries. As Aimee heard from her neighbors, who were from Jamaica and Ghana, about the challenges they face in finding water to drink, she was embarrassed to admit that in the United States even her toilet uses potable water. That got her thinking about recycling water in her own house. Now she keeps a bucket in her bathtub that catches the water that runs as she waits for warm water, as well as the excess water that falls as she showers. She then pours that water into the toilet bowl to flush. "It only saves one flush—or maybe two—each day, but at least the water gets used twice. And it's a start."

FAITH MATTERS

To the thirsty I will give water as a gift from the spring of the water of life.
REVELATION 21:6

When you turn on the tap today or take a sip of water, offer a prayer of thanks for the gift of water and offer a prayer of concern for those who don't have water today.

Stop Purchasing Bottled Water

If we want to really impact global water use, we must consider not only our own personal consumption of water but also global water consumption patterns. We need to ask questions such as: who owns the water in various parts of the world and what does our consumption of bottled water support? Has a local community's water been privatized by a large corporation and then sold to us in disposable plastic bottles simply for our convenience? How might that community suffer from not having access to, or public control over, their water? Who is impacted by the production of the plastic? Where does the plastic end up? We need to make some choices, and thus some changes, in how the world's water is controlled and consumed.

How To's

1 **Refuse to buy individual water bottles.** The water they contain is neither safer nor cleaner than most tap water, and yet water bottles are a consumer item being sold for major profits, which hastens the corporate control of the world's water sources. Bottled water is not regulated or tested the way tap water is, and it costs as much if not more than gasoline. In addition, fossil fuel energy is used both in the transportation of bottled water and in the production of new plastic. Finally, the disposal of the plastic bottles after use adds to environmental degradation.

2 **Choose a stainless steel reusable water bottle**—for your bike, lunchbox, or on the go. You can clean these bottles easily for reuse.

3 **Encourage your church to return to the old "pitcher and glasses" method of serving water.** Many churches are finding that going back to pitchers, large coolers, and individual cups are a better way to quench thirst without all the pitfalls of bottled water.

4 **Be on guard against attempts by global water corporations to privatize your town's local water resources.** Local communities around the world have realized that privatization often means less public input and oversight as well as more public cost.

Walking the Talk

Presbyterians for Restoring Creation, a national environmental organization in the Presbyterian Church (U.S.A.), went bottled-water free at its June 2005 national conference and hasn't looked back. Now PRC does not provide bottled water at any of its conferences, events, or meetings. It also encourages local churches and governing bodies to go back to pitchers and cups and leave the bottled water craze behind. For more on the PRC's bottled water campaign, go to http://www.prcweb.org.

FAITH MATTERS

Is it not enough for you to feed on the good pasture, but you must tread down with your feet the rest of your pasture? When you drink of clear water, must you foul the rest with your feet?

EZEKIEL 34:18

WATER

We all live in a particular bioregion with particular concerns related to air, land, water, and other natural systems. The watershed in which you live will have concerns specific to your region depending on whether you live in an arid or humid climate, whether you have lakes or streams or an ocean nearby, and where the highest and lowest points of land are in your area. When rain falls, how does it run? To what bodies of water do your streams run? Are there underground aquifers in your bioregion? These and other questions are important to explore when considering your local impact on your watershed.

How To's

1 **Learn about your watershed online.** Go to http://www.epa .gov/owow/watershed to learn about watershed maintenance as well as to locate your particular watershed.

2 **Contact local watershed/rivers/waterways networks or alliances** in your state to find out if they have study guides or workshops for learning about your watershed. Attend a workshop yourself or consider hosting one in your neighborhood or at your congregation. Local networks can be located at http://www.epa .gov/owow/watershed once you find your own watershed.

3 **Purchase a water quality testing kit** and go to a nearby stream, creek, pond, or lake to test the water. Once you learn the results, write up your findings in an editorial for your local paper, or create an educational display for your congregation.

4 **Find out from your local utility what kinds of processing it does for tap water** and what its challenges are. What kinds of minerals, chemicals, or other deposits are removed from your water? How does this compare to water processing in other parts of the country?

5 **Plan an outdoor activity for your congregation with a local environmental educator** who can lead a field trip of sorts to explain what your watershed is, how water flows into and out of it, and what difference each person's use of water makes.

Walking the Talk

First Presbyterian Church of Kirkwood, Missouri, hosts an annual stream cleanup as a way to care about creation and to learn about the local watershed. This intergenerational, outdoor project teaches church members about what people dispose of in the waterways in their region and what harm could come from the debris. In past years, they have found a variety of unusual objects including, literally, a kitchen sink!

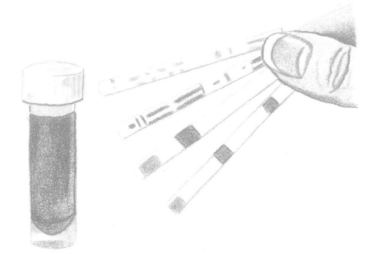

FAITH MATTERS

Wherever the river goes, every living creature that swarms will live, and there will be very many fish, once these waters reach there. It will become fresh; and everything will live where the river goes.

EZEKIEL 47:9

Live within the Limits of Your Watershed

Depending on where you live, you may have rainfall that is too little, too much, or "just right." While some plants and animals can adapt to various amounts of water in a local watershed, most of us do not limit our use of water depending on rainfall (unless local laws have been passed to impose limits and fines). Learning to live within the means of the local watershed will go a long way in helping us to preserve decreasing water supplies around the world. While some may live in water-rich areas and think their efforts don't matter, the truth is that the water system is global and that when we consume water from one part of the world, it will affect another part.

How To's

1 Learn what plants are native to your bioregion and plant them around your home or on your church's grounds instead of invasive grasses, flowers, and trees. Native plants are better adapted to grow with the amount of rain typical in your area, which means you can water less.

2 If you are reworking your driveways or parking lots, **use gravel instead of pavement**. Gravel absorbs water, while pavement creates moving runoff that overloads local water systems.

3 **Choose a day to do a stream or pond cleanup,** either on your own property or at a local park.

4 **Create a "rain garden"** where there are paved areas (walkways, driveways) or areas where a lot of water flows (such as at the end of drainpipes from gutters). Rain gardens are landscaped depressions of native plantings that help to absorb storm water runoff from impervious surfaces.

5 **Have less lawn to water.** Landscape instead with native plants.

Walking the Talk

When Door Creek Church in Madison, Wisconsin, was first built on a hilltop, the pond below it was intended to collect and filter water from the church. However, the pond became filled with trash from construction and had serious erosion problems. Church members planted the pond with native plants to beautify it and to help with erosion control. It is now a peaceful and beautiful place, with a memorial tree and a boulder inscribed with Scripture to mark the spiritual and environmental endeavors of this congregation.

Models from various Jewish, Catholic, evangelical, and mainline Protestant congregations can be found at the Web site of the National Religious Partnership for the Environment: http://www.nrpe.org.

FAITH MATTERS

Great and holy Creator, we know that you call good all that you create. You have placed us here to grow, just as the plants around us send down roots. Help us to become who you call us to be in this particular ecological neighborhood, to live and to use resources in ways that honor you, to uphold your creation, and to enable future life to flourish. Amen.

Not only is conserving water important, but so is cleaning up water that has been fouled. The products we personally use to clean (bleach?) go down our drains to join water runoff from our lawns and gardens (pesticides?). Then our personal water waste joins with whatever industry produces (sludge?) or agriculture puts out (hog waste?). From ocean liner waste to mining by-products to chemical contamination, much of the water that is being consumed is also being polluted so that it cannot return to the water cycle as it normally would. For instance, we have created "dead zones" in the Gulf of Mexico from all the agricultural chemicals that have flowed down streams to the Mississippi and then into the gulf. Also whales, polar bears, walruses, fish, coral, and other sea creatures are battling not only the impact of climate change on the seas but also the pollution of our water. Finally, the largest landfill in the world (90 percent of which is plastic) is in the middle of the Pacific Ocean. One of its two main "garbage patches" (places in the ocean where the various debris accumulates) exists between Hawaii and California and is twice the size of Texas.[4]

How To's

1 **Find alternative cleaning and pest reduction solutions** that are environmentally friendly. Homemade household cleaners include baking soda, vinegar, castille soap, and lemon. Organic gardening books, Web sites, and experts at gardening stores are good sources of information on effective, natural ways to keep pests away.

2 **Watch what you put down the drain.** While your local water utility will treat the water you put down the drain, household chemicals, lawn chemicals, and pharmaceuticals can still end up contaminating local water sources. Do not empty unknown chemicals into sinks or toilets. Many municipalities have regular disposal programs for these types of waste.

3 **Watch what others are pouring down the drain!** Find out what the local policies are regarding corporate responsibility for water pollution. How are industries held accountable for their by-products?

4 **Test your local water** and find out if there are harmful chemicals that should not be there. Talk with your local utility about where they may be coming from and if there are laws in place to prevent future pollution.

Walking the Talk

At Oberlin College's Adam Lewis Center for Environmental Studies, water is treated on site through a "living machine" and returned to the building or grounds for nonpotable sources. This wastewater treatment is actually a system of natural environments that allow plants, insects, snails, and microbes to do the biological work of cleaning the water. Rather than adding more chemicals to clean this water and consuming energy as a large wastewater treatment plant would, this living machine does the work naturally, in a beautiful atmosphere.

5 **Join a local water group** to participate in activities such as cleaning up streams or holding polluters accountable.

6 Avoid plastics. Plastic does not biodegrade; it only breaks up into smaller pieces and continues to pollute our water

FAITH MATTERS

The wilderness and the dry land shall be glad, the desert shall rejoice and blossom; like the crocus it shall blossom abundantly, and rejoice with joy and singing.

ISAIAH 35:1–2

When we do our part to protect and restore God's creation, then all creation can delight as God intends.

Advocate for Effective Water Policies

After learning about our impact locally and globally, we can make changes in our own lifestyles while we also work to influence larger systems. While our consumptive choices will shape global water use, our engaged public policy advocacy may have more far-reaching consequences for sustainable water usage worldwide. We can advocate for municipally controlled water or regulated water systems, for fair agricultural water policies, for city conservation policies, and more.

How To's

1 Know your legislators—both nationally and locally. To find your elected officials, go to http://www.usa.gov/Contact/Elected.shtml.

2 Communicate with your legislators. Make visits to their offices, send letters, and make phone calls to express your opinions and values.

3 Make use of the media. Write letters to the editor of the local paper on current environmental debates and concerns. Invite the press if you are organizing a rally or hosting a popular educational event. Comment on legislators' commitments to God's creation (or lack thereof).

4 Educate yourself. Learn what issues are being discussed in the halls of power. You can track national policy discussions through various denominational offices in Washington, D.C. (Many links to such offices can be found on the Web site of the National Council of Churches' Eco-Justice Program: http://www.nccecojustice.org/links.htm.)

When communicating with legislators, be sure that you know the issue and the specific bill name and number (if there is one), and be clear about why you care, including how the issue relates to your local concerns and/or to your faith.

Walking the Talk

The World Council of Churches has an Ecumenical Water Network (http://www.oikoumene.org/?id=2958). This network has been created by Christians around the world in order "to make a Christian witness heard in the present debate on water issues, to raise awareness of churches and to engage as an ecumenical community in common action at all levels." The Ecumenical Water Network is a way for Christians to learn about how others around the world are advocating for effective policies and political changes for better water decisions.

5 **Educate others!** Once you know more, share your knowledge of current issues, key players, and upcoming policy discussions with others. Host an educational event to share your biblical and theological commitments to care for creation, and provide information about what is happening in your area. Invite elected officials or local environmental leaders to speak about their efforts.

6 **Focus your communication on particular issues.** Rather than sharing general environmental concern, communicate your passion about specific water concerns (such as water conservation, water ownership, water use, and water waste). One such vital issue is protecting the local water supply from industrial pollutants and from agricultural runoff through stricter water waste regulations for industry.

FAITH MATTERS

Morning Has Broken

Sweet the rain's new fall, sunlit from heaven,
Like the first dewfall, on the first grass.
Praise for the sweetness of the wet garden,
Sprung in completeness where God's feet pass.

Celebrate Water!

Sometimes when we check items off our environmental "to do" lists, we forget that we are engaged in these lifestyle changes because of our joy and appreciation for God's great and glorious work. Our response to the beauty of creation is thankfulness, and that thankfulness is embodied in our action. Don't turn off the faucet because of guilt or compulsion but because you are convicted that it is a way to be thankful and responsible.

How To's

1 **Host a summer water party,** serving water as the beverage of choice (with or without ice) in fancy glasses. Eat water-laden fruits and vegetables (melons are particularly good). Engage in water activities such as playing scales on glasses of water filled to different levels, painting with watercolors, splashing around in a pool or sprinkler, and making colorful "reminder" signs with water conservation tips for guests to take home.

2 **Worship with water.** Set aside a worship service in your congregation to celebrate God's gift of water. This can be done in conjunction with a baptism, a renewal of baptism, or simply by focusing on the theme of water through Scripture, preaching, and liturgy. Scripture has wonderful stories of water, and our religious tradition is rich with theological meaning for water. Include the arts, children, music, and fun as you plan this special worship service.

3 **Plan a day of limited water use followed by a day of celebration.** For the first day, shut off the water from the house or building and give everyone a small bucket of water for doing the things they need to do that day—cleaning, bathing, washing dishes, flushing the toilet. Have one clean pitcher of water for drinking that people can share. Make a chart for how long it took people to use up the water in their buckets, and talk about what it is like to have limited water. The second day, turn the water on in the house. Go to each faucet in the house and say a prayer or blessing over the water such as "God, we praise you for the gift of water, and we promise to not take this water for granted. Please be present with those who have limited water and help us to always be conscious not to waste this gift."

Walking the Talk

Congregations from different denominations located within the Chesapeake Bay watershed decided to form a group to protect the bay's special ecosystem. The network exists to "establish healing ministries for lands and waters, to revere and cherish God's creation, and restore the ability of the Chesapeake Bay to sustain a diversity of life." More than twenty churches began this ecumenical movement, and they now gather together at conferences and other meetings to meet their goal of being "God's partners in the restoration of this beloved watershed." To learn more go to http://www.nccecojustice.org/cheshome.htm.

FAITH MATTERS

Jesus said to her, "Everyone who drinks of this water will be thirsty again, but those who drink of the water that I will give them will never be thirsty. The water that I will give will become in them a spring of water gushing up to eternal life."

JOHN 4:13–14

5. PEOPLE

It is because of human activities that
we are in an accelerated period of
climate change. Yet while people are the
reason we are in this unprecedented time
for the planet, people are also suffering
greatly from the effects of climate change.
Whether the effect is the rise in sea level,
increased floods and droughts, harsher
natural storms and disasters, or the
precarious food situation, climate change
is changing human lives and livelihoods.
It particularly impacts those who are
more vulnerable because of age, race,
socioeconomic status, or living condition.

PEOPLE

All people are affected by climate change. Yet not all are affected to the same degree. Those who are already more vulnerable in our world—because of poverty, hunger, or oppression—are the ones who suffer most from the effects of climate change. Environmental destruction has long had a correlation to race and class. The term "environmental justice" describes a movement to ensure that environmental ills and benefits are distributed evenly among the population rather than being concentrated in ways that reflect society's ongoing injustices.

How To's

1 Attend environmental justice rallies. Whether in a community that is feeling the effects of pesticide applications in agricultural fields or in a community that is threatened by a toxic waste dump, the sad reality is that most communities have some environmental justice issues facing them. Find out who does community organizing in your area, be it against factory pollution, industrial air quality, polluted water, toxic waste, or agricultural applications. Join with them in demanding justice.

2 Lobby against toxic waste sites and other environmental hazards in poor communities and communities of color. Tell your elected representatives that vulnerable populations must not pay the price of corporations and industries that cause climate change and pollute the local neighborhood.

3 Study environmental justice in your congregation. Many resources are available, such as *Environmental Racism: An Ecumenical Study Guide* from the National Council of Churches' Eco-Justice Program Office, which is available online at http://www.nccecojustice.org/resources.html.

4 Connect local environmental justice to global environmental justice. Recognize that our greenhouse gas emissions are warming the seas on which indigenous people depend for food; are raising sea levels, which threatens island communities; and are causing increased natural disasters, which hit vulnerable people the hardest. Learn more about these populations and what relief efforts might be possible.

Walking the Talk

The United Church of Christ has long been passionate for environmental justice. In August 2004, the UCC sponsored a young adult, multiracial, multiethnic gathering on the West Coast to explore environmental racism. Young people from Puerto Rico, Nevada, and California learned about the combined economic and environmental injustices people faced along the U.S.-Mexico border and on American Indian reservations. Both leaders and participants on this trip left the experience inspired and committed to advocate for environmental justice, believing that all people have a right to enjoy the world that God created.

http://www.nrpe.org/profiles/profiles_vi_C_9_01.htm.

FAITH MATTERS

They sell the righteous for silver, and the needy for a pair of sandals—they who trample the head of the poor into the dust of the earth, and push the afflicted out of the way.

AMOS 2:6–7

PEOPLE

Childhood asthma and other environment-related illnesses are on the rise as air pollution worsens and the effects of climate change increase. When we burn fossil fuels to produce energy, we are not only making it harder for the earth to flourish but also are making it more difficult for children to breathe. Also, we are finding that many of the new products created through our modern, energy-intensive manufacturing processes contain toxins that harm children's health. Finally, harvesting our energy from coal-fired power plants releases mercury, which is another risk to children's health.[1] The Eco-Justice Program Office of the National Council of Churches reports that "children breathe 50 percent more air, drink more fluids, and eat more food in proportion to their body weight than adults. Environmental exposures that would not harm an adult can cause permanent damage to the developing body of a child."[2] The World Health Organization confirms the depth of the problem: "Over 40% of the global burden of disease attributed to environmental factors falls on children below five years of age, who account for only about 10% of the world's population."[3]

How To's

1 Fight for the passage of clean air laws, emissions standards, and renewable energy development.

2 Use the Environmental Working Group's research on best options for children from sunscreen to the safest fish to eat (http://www.ewg.org/forparents).

Walking the Talk

The California Interfaith Partnership for Children's Health and the Environment advocates for safe and healthy environmental public policies and works to educate parents, schools, and religious communities about children's environmental health. They have created flyers and lead workshops in order to help draw the connection between caring for children and caring for the earth.

http://www.nrpe.org/profiles/profiles_vi_A_18_01.htm.

3 Read *Christian Principles for a Healthy Body and Spirit,* a document drawn up by a coalition of faith-based eco-justice groups, at http://www.nccecojustice.org/ehprinciples.html.

4 Form a small group at your congregation or in your community to study environmental health through a faith-based resource. For suggestions of study guides and videos, go to http://www.nccecojustice.org/envirohealthresources.htm.

5 Reduce your indoor air pollution and inquire about indoor air quality at your local school. Look for proper ventilation, test for mold and radon, and know what chemicals are in the carpet, paint, walls, ceilings, and furniture. To learn more go to http://www.epa.gov/iaq/index.html. .

FAITH MATTERS

And the king will answer them, "Truly I tell you, just as you did it to one of the least of these who are members of my family, you did it to me."

MATTHEW 25:40

When natural disasters and severe storms occur, it is the world's most vulnerable populations that are hit the hardest and have the worst time recovering. From mudslides in Guatemala to tsunamis in the Indian Ocean, from droughts in Africa to earthquakes in China, from hurricanes in the southeastern United States to flooding in the Midwest, the populations who are already affected by poverty, hunger, poor health, or limited resources are always more greatly impacted by natural disaster. One of the long-predicted effects of climate change is an increase in frequency and/or an increase in severity of natural disasters and storms.

How To's

1 **Pay attention to natural disasters.** Most individual weather events will not be exclusively connected by scientists to climate change, because the science of climate change deals with broader patterns and overall changes, not singular weather events. However, if we are to understand what the impacts of an increase in storm frequency and severity might mean for us—socially, economically, culturally, and environmentally—we can begin by tracking the effects of current disasters.

 Pray for those who are hardest hit in disasters.

 Volunteer to help with rebuilding or relief efforts where possible. Most denominations have disaster assistance or relief offices that can connect you to volunteer opportunities.

4 **Donate financial resources** to relief efforts.

Walking the Talk

Episcopal Relief and Development believes that good assistance can mitigate the effects of climate change while also mitigating the effects of hunger, poverty, disease, and disasters. In addition to providing immediate relief for natural disasters, ERD will also work to enable local people to cope long-term with environmental risks. Forestry programs, smokeless stoves, and agricultural assistance are examples of the ways ERD helps communities, families, and individuals cope with soil erosion, hunger, drought, and respiratory infections—all dangers that are made worse by global climate change.

http://ecusa.anglican.org/erd/newsroom_97627_ENG_HTM.htm.

FAITH MATTERS

[Jesus] said to him, "'You shall love the Holy One your God with all your heart, and with all your soul, and with all your mind.' This is the greatest and first commandment. And a second is like it: 'You shall love your neighbor as yourself.' On these two commandments hang all the law and the prophets."

MATTHEW 22:37–40

Consider Overpopulation and Overconsumption

Because global climate change is anthropogenic (caused by human activities), the more humans there are, the worse the problem will be. Unfortunately, overpopulation is already a key concern, and it is unlikely that we will see a reverse trend any time soon. From 5 million people worldwide in 8,000 BCE we now are nearly 6 billion people. The most rapid population growth in history occurred in the last hundred years.[4] Effects of overpopulation include deforestation and other unsustainable methods of consumption of natural resources, as well as hunger and poverty.[5] While overpopulation itself is an eco-justice concern, so also are consumption rates per person. All people need basic resources to survive, so any increase in population increases the demands on the earth. However, some of us use an extravagant amount of resources not just to survive but to live lifestyles that are unsustainable in the long run. Consumption per person has grown most rapidly in so-called developed nations. On average, if people lived as most U.S. citizens do, we would need multiple Earths to support the population.

How To's

 1 **Learn more about overpopulation** and its impacts on other species and natural systems.

2 **Test your ecological footprint** at http://www .myfootprint.org/en or another similar Web site to see what your lifestyle requires of the earth. Understand that we each are responsible for our own lifestyle choices but that we also bear responsibility for some of our corporate decisions regarding resource use, infrastructure, and energy use.

3 **Reduce your personal consumption** to live only on the recommended sustainable footprint level of forty-three acres.[6]

4 **Support agencies working to provide family planning and reproductive health services** to people around the world who desire it.

 5 **Consider adoption** as a way to add new members to your family.

Walking the Talk

Susan Power Bratton, chair of environmental studies at Baylor University, wrote a book titled *Six Billion and More: Human Population Regulation and Christian Ethics.* In this book, Bratton urges Christians to learn how to apply theology, ethics, and Christian values to the issue of overpopulation. Because the conversation can become complicated—particularly around issues of abortion, coercion, and justice—it is vital that people of faith learn how to articulate their beliefs and their ethical boundaries faithfully.

FAITH MATTERS

God, our Great Creator, we confess that we listen too readily to your command in Genesis to "be fruitful and multiply" without realizing that you gave this command first to creatures of sea and sky. We know that we have multiplied to the point where other species are made extinct and your earth groans for relief. Help us, O God, to be more humble in understanding our true needs, and more ready to help those who desire family planning services. In Christ we pray for your guidance and wisdom. Amen.

PEOPLE

"Living wage" campaigns (to demand fair wages rather than minimum wages), affordable housing advocacy, and global antipoverty initiatives end up helping people care for the world's resources. When communities are impoverished and have no other resources or outside help, they may feel their only option is to use the natural resources around them, even if the resultant deforestation, soil erosion, or pollution may in the long run harm their health and that of creation. When people are given more economic possibilities, they are able to care more for their environment and to empower others to do so.

How To's

1. **Study national trade policies.** Learn what standards are applied to U.S. companies in the United States and around the world. Find out who benefits most and who is most negatively impacted. Most denominational offices in Washington, D.C., have resources for studying the issue of trade, and U.S. senators and representatives will often include their stances on their Web sites.

2. **Host an adult study** to discuss the biblical principles and values that should guide economic decisions. Check your denomination's economic justice, hunger, or peacemaking office for resources.

3. **Advocate for just trade policies.** Because most denominations have taken a strong stance on what constitutes trade that is fair and just, you may be able to advocate through your faith community.

4. **Advocate for affordable housing and the institution of a "living" wage** in your community. For more information on the living wage campaign, see http://www .letjusticeroll.org.

5. **Purchase fair-trade products**—items that have been produced with just conditions and fair wages for all workers along the line. Fair-trade coffee, tea, chocolate, and other food items are available as well as fair-trade clothing,

Walking the Talk

RELUFA is a national network of churches and nonprofit organizations in Cameroon that addresses economic injustice. Two of the major projects of this network respond to the failure of adequate compensation to residents during the construction of the Chad-Cameroon oil pipeline and the negative impact of the global economy on the people of Cameroon. In addition to education and advocacy about the pipeline, RELUFA offers small, low-interest loans to local populations, teaching them about finance and bringing relief to their own situations. Supported by the presbyteries of Chicago and of the Twin Cities Area, and facilitated by PCUSA mission coworker Christi Boyd, this network makes vital connections between economic and environmental justice. For more information, see http://relufa.org/reception.htm or http://www.pcusa.org/joininghands/cameroon.htm.

crafts, instruments, decorations, toys, and more. Check out large fair-trade providers such as SERRV International (http://www.serrv.org) or Ten Thousand Villages (http://www.tenthousandvillages.com).

6 **Participate in the Fair Trade Coffee Project.** Most mainline Protestant denominations have national projects connecting thousands of congregations to the issue of fair trade through selling and serving good coffee that provides a fair wage for coffee growers around the world. Find out how to participate at http://www.equalexchange.com/interfaith-program.

FAITH MATTERS

For a while he refused; but later he said to himself, "Though I have no fear of God and no respect for anyone, yet because this widow keeps bothering me, I will grant her justice, so that she may not wear me out by continually coming."

LUKE 18:4–5

PEOPLE

War exacerbates hunger, poverty, and environmental degradation. Fighting tactics have long included salting an enemy's fields so they are no longer arable, destroying community wells, or slaughtering livestock needed by the community to survive. Whether the environmental concern is chemical warfare, the energy used in manufacturing weapons, the fuel used by machinery, or the actual physical destruction of people, animals, and the environment, militarization and warfare impact climate change and many other social, economic, and environmental justice concerns.

How To's

1 **Research the connections between war and environmental destruction.** What tactics most hurt people and the earth? Why are these tactics used? What environmental health concerns are left in the wake of war? What parts of the local ecology can recover? What aspects of warfare might make climate change worse?

2 **Contact elected officials** and share your views. Advocate for policies that help war-torn countries recover their local ecology. Also, advocate for energy efficiency, renewable energy, and other ways to limit the consumption of energy at U.S. military schools and bases. Finally, advocate for the funding of programs that build peace (e.g., development assistance, UN peacekeepers, reconciliation programs, diplomacy).

3 **Work for peaceful resolutions** to conflicts. The less military intervention, the better for all God's creation.

4 **Participate in the International Day of Prayer for Peace.** To learn more, see http://www.overcomingviolence.org/index.php?id=1487.

Walking the Talk

The Fellowship of Reconciliation, one of the oldest interfaith peace organizations in the United States, exists to help people learn about peacemaking and nonviolence. Its May 2008 newsletter lifted up the peace work of an Iranian couple cycling around the world in order to promote peace and protect the environment. Traveling on bicycles and planting trees in cities all around the world, Nasim and Jafar contributed to interfaith efforts of peace.

FAITH MATTERS

Bloodshed follows bloodshed. Therefore the land mourns, and all who live in it languish.

HOSEA 4:2–3

PEOPLE

Education, advocacy, and volunteer work are crucial to caring for all people, particularly the most vulnerable, in God's creation. Yet our efforts to care for and about people should not feel like work or like an obligation. Building community to care for creation should be fun! Being with other people, working to curb climate change and create peace, should be a kind of jubilee. Restoring relationship with others is part of our human vocation.

How To's

1 **Enjoy your neighbors.** Harken back to the "olden days" of front-porch swings, multiple yards occupied with children's games, intergenerational storytelling, and backyard barbeques. Create a block party or a small neighbors' party to get to know one another and have fun. Make sure all people are included.

2 **Pray for your neighbors** as well as for people you don't know across town and around the world. Give thanks for the way their lives enrich your life.

3 **Create a partnership between your congregation and a church in another part of the city,** to get to know and care about one another and the issues you each face. Get together for fun community events and build relationships based on hope and friendship.

4 **Build community in worship.** During a communal prayer time, spread a world map on a table or the floor and invite people to come forward, light tea candles, and place them on communities on the map that are especially vulnerable to climate change or communities that are doing marvelous work to help God's creation.

5 **Form a "creation care team" or "green group"** at your church to give one another support and to work on curbing climate change together. Be sure to plan time for celebration and community fun in addition to serious environmental plans.

Walking the Talk

Global gatherings of Christians help church members around the world learn about one another and the social and environmental problems they face. In the Stewards program of the World Alliance of Reformed Churches, young people assist at General Council meetings while talking on the sidelines about poverty, greed, environmental destruction, war, and natural disasters. Mixing friendship and work, politics and theology, fun and prayer concerns, these young adults grow to understand all the concerns that link social and environmental justice. In a safe environment, relationships are formed across national boundaries, creating community around the globe.

FAITH MATTERS

God, we recognize the devastation that climate change wreaks across the globe, particularly for people who are vulnerable because of age, poverty, or other living situations. We know you care for all your people and that our actions affect people's lives. Guide us in your good wisdom to honor all people so that we might curb climate change together and find justice for all.

6. OTHE

Sometimes the study of climate change leads us to think first about human suffering or large geological shifts. Humans do feel the effects strongly, and there are indeed large movements occurring in oceans, deserts, and the hydrological cycle. Yet other species are intimately affected by all of these changes as well. Whether the focus is on ocean coral dying or on trees that can no longer survive the shifting seasonal boundaries, species other than Homo sapiens are feeling the adverse effects of climate change. Their protection is part of the action needed to curb the worst effects of climate change. By creating habitats and protecting species, we work to develop some of the same attitudes, values, and actions that are needed to curb climate change.

SPECIES

OTHER SPECIES

Scientists have informed us that we are in the sixth period of mass extinction. Like global climate change, this particular mass extinction is being caused by human activities. As rural and wilderness areas are developed by human hands, as natural systems are polluted by industry, as native species are threatened by invasive species, and as animals are harvested for food at alarming rates, more and more species are becoming threatened, endangered, and extinct. As sea levels rise and ocean temperatures warm, coral, polar bears, penguins, and other animals not considered endangered are now at risk of becoming so.

Scientists estimate that over five hundred species of plants and animals have gone extinct in the United States in the past two hundred years.

Only 1,200 species in the United States are officially listed as threatened or endangered, while scientists believe there are 6,500 species at risk of extinction.

According to the U.S. Fish and Wildlife Service, the Endangered Species Act has saved 99.3 percent of its listed species from extinction.[1]

How To's

1 Find out which species are threatened or endangered. The U.S. Fish and Wildlife Service has a Web site where you can find out various listings for your state, the country, and other countries: http://www.fws.gov/Endangered/wildlife.html.

2 Work with children on an art project that includes pictures, drawings, or sculptures of threatened, endangered, or extinct animals in order to create interest and empathy. Download an endangered species coloring book from http://www.epa.gov/espp/coloring.

3 Learn about animals and appreciate them. Visit the zoo, a local forest, or a conservation area to observe animals. Learning about animal behavior is a great way to build environmental empathy and interest in children.

4 Pray for the endangered animals in your region.

Walking the Talk

The Noah Alliance assists Jewish, evangelical, mainline Protestant, and other religious communities to advocate for endangered species through providing sermon starters, curriculum materials, songs, and other resources. In 2005 and 2006, this organization worked to protect the Endangered Species Act when it was under the threat of being weakened in Congress. For more information or to use their resources, go to http://www.noahalliance.org.

5 **Support policies that preserve natural habitats** for wild animals, insects, and plants as well as policies that curb the tendency to develop new areas for suburban sprawl.

6 **Adopt a species.** Through a conservation organization such as the World Wildlife Fund (https://secure.worldwildlife.org/ogc), find a way to "adopt" a threatened or endangered species.

7 **Read denominational statements about biodiversity.** Find out what your denomination says about biodiversity from your church's national offices, or check out different denominational statements at http://www.nccecojustice.org/anthohome.htm.

FAITH MATTERS

Then God said to Noah and to his sons with him, "As for me, I am establishing my covenant with you and your descendants after you, and with every living creature that is with you, the birds, the domestic animals, and every animal of the earth with you, as many as came out of the ark."

GENESIS 9:8–10

In the last few decades, the use of toxic pesticides has increased drastically. Because toxic pesticides are intended to kill pests, and because these pesticides usually do not discriminate in species, pesticides can affect the health of your local land and water when they leach into the soil or make their way to local streams during storms. Pesticides can also make children sick if breathed in too heavily, absorbed through the skin, or accidentally ingested. Meanwhile, organic gardening and natural ways to reduce pests are possible (using ingredients like soap, skim milk, or stinging nettles).

How To's

1 **Care for your garden or lawn organically.** Pests can often be kept away by beneficial insects, birds, and even by some plants they do not like the taste or smell of. Physical obstacles such as fencing or netting will also reduce pests. Finally, there are some natural mixtures that can be sprayed on plants to help protect them. Your local garden store should have a host of resources to learn organic gardening and lawn maintenance.

2 **Research concerns linked to pesticide use.** Search for products, chemical ingredients, or nontoxic alternatives through the pesticide database at http://pesticideinfo.org.

3 **Advocate for better testing and research of pesticides.** One good resource for advocacy or campaigning is the Pesticide Action Network of North America (http://www.panna.org).

4 **Purchase "pesticide free zone" signs** to hang at your home, church, or school once you have eliminated the use of pesticides. Look under "merchandise" at http://www.pesticidefreezone.org.

5 **Choose insect repellent that is safer for children and the environment.** Search for products recommended by the Environmental Working Group at http://www.cosmeticsdatabase.com.

Walking the Talk

Seminarians at San Francisco Theological Seminary engage their bodies in theology and ethics by working in the "pesticide free zone" on campus—their seminary garden. This cooperative effort, facilitated by Christian ethics professor Carol Robb, is a way for students to connect care for the earth with their ministry. Picking slugs off plants, building mechanical barriers to keep strawberries safe, and weeding by hand are activities that provide good exercise and connection to God's creation and that keep petrochemical pesticides out of this garden. Students enjoy the aesthetics of this bountiful garden as well as the tasty vegetables it produces as they learn to appreciate all the bright and beautiful things that God has made.

FAITH MATTERS

All Things Bright and Beautiful
Each little flower that opens,
Each little bird that sings,
God made their growing colors,
God made their tiny wings.

All things bright and beautiful,
All creatures great and small,
All things wise and wonderful:
Our dear God made them all.

OTHER SPECIES

By now we might be accustomed to seeing green grass in desert regions, mowed lawn in prairie landscapes, and kudzu growing all over the southeastern United States. The danger of invasive species is that different geographical and geological regions need differently adapted species to participate in the local ecosystem. Driving cross-country should not only present drastically different features—mountains, valleys, seashores, forests, deserts, and prairies—but also a variety of the plants that grow in these diverse landscapes. Exotic grasses and plants, often promoted in past generations for reasons of aesthetic pleasure or assumed horticultural benefit, are now often considered weeds. Exotic species can drive out native species, which are better suited to harmonize with other species in the ecosystem. New efforts are taking place across the country to reintroduce native plants to our lands and to remove invasive species.

How To's

1 Learn what invasive species are particularly problematic in your area. Your county extension office should be able to give you information and help you find further resources for study.

2 Keep invasive species out of your area. Look at the plants proposed for your home, office, or church landscape and know where they are from and how they will work in your bioregion.

3 Volunteer for a habitat restoration project. For ways to volunteer, see the National Invasive Species Information Center at http://www .invasivespeciesinfo.gov/news /whatyou.shtml.

4 Nurture native plants in your home or church garden.

Walking the Talk

Members of the Lutheran Church of the Reformation in St. Louis Park, Minnesota, decided to do their part in protecting biodiversity by landscaping their church grounds with native plants. In order to restore the prairie land species that are native to the area, they had to dig up nice green lawn and even a few large trees. In their place they planted native grasses as well as some bur oaks. Their project was visible because the land they restored to native plantings was highway frontage, and they now have visitors—human, avian, and insect—who come by the church to enjoy the wildflowers and native grasses.

FAITH MATTERS

And the Holy God planted a garden in Eden, in the east; and there God put the human whom God had formed. Out of the ground the Holy God made to grow every tree that is pleasant to the sight and good for food, the tree of life also in the midst of the garden, and the tree of the knowledge of good and evil.

GENESIS 2:8–9

Watch What You Eat

The foods we raise, consume, and ship around the world require vast energy and natural resources. In addition, they also impact local ecosystems. Natural balance is overturned in streams, lakes, and oceans when we consume more fish than can be reproduced naturally. Also, genetically engineered crops raised for consumption influence wild plants, upsetting biodiversity. Finally, factory farming and industrial agriculture reduce the varieties and types of produce and animals and limit the genetic diversity that used to exist around the globe.

How To's

1 **Eat your fruits and veggies!** Eating lower on the food chain saves energy and other resources. When you eat a variety of grains, fruits, and veggies, you will diversify both your diet and the animal kingdom.

2 **Try to buy "simple" foods.** If the ingredients list includes a lot of ingredients you don't recognize, try to choose a simpler item.

3 **Buy dolphin-safe tuna** if you eat tuna.

4 If you buy animal products for food, **buy meats that are marked as antibiotic-free, grain-fed, and free-range, or buy from a local farmer** whom you trust.

5 **Know what fish to avoid** in your region. Check the seafood guide created by the Monterey Bay Aquarium to know which fish to eat: http://www.mbayaq.org/cr/SeafoodWatch/web/sfw _regional.aspx.

6 **Buy local foods** at your local store or at farmers' markets, where you can talk with local farmers about their methods and beliefs in farming.

7 **Cultivate and/or buy heirloom foods.** Heirlooms preserve unique species that otherwise would rapidly be crowded out by the cultivation of just one kind of each food. For heirloom meats, one source is http://www.heritagefoodsusa.com. Many local gardening stores have heirloom seeds and seedlings. Farmers' markets (and sometimes local grocers) have heirloom produce for sale.

Walking the Talk

For six years, children have come to the backyard of Crescent Hill Presbyterian Church in Louisville, Kentucky, for a gardening day camp in which they learn how to plant and harvest produce and then to make good food from those fresh fruits and vegetables. Stephen Bartlett, a church member and the organizer of the camp, says, "We have seen some of the parents of the children turn up at worship months later, and keep coming. This has helped our church look and feel more diverse socioeconomically, culturally, and racially." This camp also changes children's lives. Bartlett explains: "The idea of the garden is to demonstrate to children that the commons still exists, that if someone is hungry and needs to eat out of this garden, they can, because it is not a private space but a common community garden space. In our highly privatized society, this idea comes as something of a revelation to many of the children."

8 **Buy foods that have not been genetically engineered.** Many natural food stores, and some local groceries as well, will carry foods that are specifically marked as not including genetically engineered ingredients. Because the USDA does not require the food industry to label products that have been genetically engineered, the onus is on smaller, independent companies to specifically market and claim the non-GE label.

9 **Avoid foods from industrial agriculture or factory farms.** Most of their produce or meats are not heirloom varieties and are often genetically engineered. Complexity and diversity (both inherent in biodiversity) are not part of this corporate mentality.

FAITH MATTERS

For the fate of humans and the fate of animals is the same; as one dies, so dies the other. They all have the same breath, and humans have no advantage over the animals; for all is vanity.

ECCLESIASTES 3:19

Host a Blessing of the Animals

OTHER SPECIES

Whether for your family, your neighborhood, or your church, hosting an event like a blessing of the animals helps all involved to be aware of nonhuman creatures and to care for their welfare. Sometimes the key to acting against climate change, or to save endangered species, is to take a first step toward a better awareness and appreciation of nonhuman life. A blessing of the animals is a great way to help participants realize that God creates and loves all creatures, that all life has meaning in and of itself, and that it is a blessing and a privilege for us to benefit from the joy and affection of animals. From this first step along the road of environmental awareness and commitment, we then can take further steps toward specific actions against climate change.

How To's

1 **Decide what kind of blessing you want to host.** Will it involve a pastor? Will it be informal or formal? Where will you host it? What kinds of animals will you invite people to bring (e.g., pets, farm animals, mammals, insects)? How big will the event be? Can children be involved? Look online for models of how churches, seminaries, and other institutions have done animal blessing services.

2 **Find Scripture readings, prayers, music, and interactive elements** to help shape the event.

3 **Designate who will lead what parts of the service and who will help animals** (and their human companions) through the service.

4 **Plan for refreshment** (if needed) for both people and animals.

Walking the Talk

St. Mark's Episcopal Church in Seattle hosts an annual Blessing of the Animals on the Feast of Saint Francis. Children and adults alike bring animals to be blessed during this special worship service. Family pets, often held in the arms of children, are blessed individually while wild animals (such as migratory birds and the salmon and whales in Puget Sound) are remembered with prayers. The animals brought to worship include cats, dogs, rabbits, birds, fish, reptiles, and chickens.

FAITH MATTERS

For the Beauty of the Earth
For the beauty of the earth,
For the glory of the skies,
For the love which from our birth
Over and around us lies,
God of all, to Thee we raise
This our hymn of grateful praise.

For the wonder of each hour
Of the day and of the night,
Hill and vale, and tree and flower,
Sun and moon, and stars of light,
God of all, to Thee we raise
This our hymn of grateful praise.

Create Backyard Habitats

Why is it important to create habitat? As endangered species rise and as climate change transforms once-dependable stopping points for migratory animals (and home territories for other species), carving out wild spaces in our constantly developing world is vital to the health and well-being of all creatures. By doing your own research and being creative with your plantings, you can create a habitat to invite specific beneficial insects or animals. You can also follow the National Wildlife Federation's program, which offers specific steps for inventing backyard habitats. The organization will even offer certification for the process. The NWF's backyard habitat program is one way that you or your church can reclaim some land for other species as well as for the enjoyment humans will get out of observing those other species in a safe environment.

How To's

1 To make an appropriate habitat for wildlife, **provide four basic elements:** food, water, shelter, and a place to raise young.

2 **Use native plants.** Pollinators have often coevolved with particular plants, which is why native plants are so important to wildlife habitats.

3 Your whole community can be wildlife habitat, so **check with other interested neighbors.**

4 **Consult the NWF tip sheets** to help you create the following habitats: bird-friendly habitats, butterfly-attracting habitats, amphibian havens, habitats with ponds, bird feeders, or nesting boxes, ways to reduce your lawn.[2]

The Gardener's Guide to Global Warming, produced by the National Wildlife Federation, offers information about how your plantings could be affected by global warming. It also shows which states may find their state tree or state flower affected by the anticipated climate changes. To download this guide or to read more, go to http://www.nwf.org/gardenersguide.

Walking the Talk

In Montreat, North Carolina, dozens of residents have created backyard habitats in recent years. By April 2006, approximately thirty homes in this small community had received the official certification from the National Wildlife Federation. Montreat holds a special place in the heart of many Presbyterians because it is home to PCUSA-affiliated Montreat Conference Center and Montreat College. Because "Montreat was originally founded as a spiritual retreat, and spiritual restoration is Montreat's most important commodity" (http://www.townofmontreat.org/about.php), it makes sense that peaceful places throughout the town are provided not just for humans but for all of God's creatures.

(Montreat Board of Commissioners, "Town Council Meeting Minutes" [minutes from town of Montreat council meeting, Montreat, NC, July 13, 2006]; available at http://74.125.45.132/search?q=cache:NbGkaTl8vfwJ:www .townofmontreat.org/documents/071306BOC.pdf+montreat+backyard+wildlife+habitat&hl=en&ct=clnk&cd=3& gl=us&client=safari

FAITH MATTERS

Praise the Holy One from the earth, you sea monsters and all deeps, fire and hail, snow and frost, stormy wind fulfilling God's command! Mountains and all hills, fruit trees and all cedars! Wild animals and all cattle, creeping things and flying birds!

PSALM 148:7–10

Enjoy God's Creation

Animal behavior is fascinating. Plant life can be surprising. Whether it is on educational television or on a safari, it is worthwhile to take time to absorb and enjoy the world around you. Standing on a mountaintop or gazing up at the night sky, it is helpful sometimes to feel how small we are compared with the world. God calls good all that God creates. God delights in the world and invites us also to delight in the world. We can learn a lot about instinct, patterns, relationships, and life from other species. They can teach us about ourselves. Certainly they can point to the Creator.

How To's

1 **Take a walk,** quieting your mind from daily business and focusing instead on the natural world, pausing to observe anything that catches your interest.

2 **Hang bird feeders and/or a bird bath** by windows where you have a favorite chair. Spend a few minutes every day watching and enjoying the birds.

3 **Nurture plants,** indoors or outdoors, and enjoy their startling growth, their life cycles, and their responses to the environment around them.

4 **Plan a group hike** in a local park or forest with a naturalist to learn what flora and fauna exist in your local ecosystem.

5 **Visit your local nature center or zoo** to learn about endangered animals, threatened habitat, and what work can be done to help.

6 **Host a film festival or community viewing of nature shows or animal videos.** Invite children to dress up as their favorite plant or animal. Serve snacks that match the theme.

Walking the Talk

In 2008, Manassas Church of the Brethren in Manassas, Virginia, won the National Council of Churches' Eco-Justice Program's Green Congregation Award for Children's Ministry for its Jr. BUGS program. In this congregation, BUGS means "Better Understanding of Green Stewardship," and the Jr. BUGS program teaches children how they can help care for and enjoy God's creation. As they explore ways to care for creation, they earn badges with fun names such as "Wanda Worm" (for attending to worms and other critters that help in the compost bin) and "Lucy Ladybug" (for planting and caring for seeds in the church garden).

FAITH MATTERS

But ask the animals, and they will teach you; the birds of the air, and they will tell you; ask the plants of the earth, and they will teach you; and the fish of the sea will declare to you.

JOB 12:7–8

7. WILDERNESS

Wilderness areas are disappearing as land becomes commercially developed, as population grows, and as climate change alters the life cycles of plants and animals. The disappearing of wilderness areas not only has spiritual consequences for those of us who find God revealed in particular ways in undeveloped areas, but it also has real consequences for our future. Without forests to help mediate carbon emissions and cool temperatures (particularly in the tropics), and without wide swaths of other landscapes where pavement, buildings, and industry are absent, climate change will accelerate.

AND LAND

WILDERNESS AND LAND

This is not a suggestion that everyone should go plant a tree in the backyard. Depending on where you live and why you're planting the tree, you may not have the impact on climate change that you desire. In any place, protecting current forests and old-growth trees is beneficial. In addition, individually planted trees on your property can shade windows (reducing energy use inside), provide habitat for wildlife, and add beauty to the property. While planting new trees that are native to, and sustainable in, a particular region will help with soil erosion, desertification, and local wood needs, not all tree planting necessarily will help cool the planet. Trees absorb carbon dioxide and produce oxygen, and they evaporate water and keep things cool (just think of walking into a forest on a sunny day). However, in temperate zones the effect of adding more dark canopy may absorb (rather than reflect) the sun's rays and could actually lead to a kind of warming affect.[1] (In tropical zones, however, planting trees should help to slow climate change.)

How To's

1 Support organizations working to stop deforestation. Protecting current forests, particularly rain forests, is crucial.

2 If you want to plant a new tree in your garden, on your lawn, or on your church grounds, check with your county extension or a local arborist for advice as to when and how to plant in your region and what trees are recommended for your purpose.

3 Research movements to plant trees and find out where they are planting (temperate or tropical), what kinds of trees they are using, and why they are planting. For instance, if trees are planted to bolster the livelihood of people living in poverty, or to bring back past biodiversity, it may be worth supporting even if such planting might be in a temperate zone and thus not necessarily help climate change.

A few tree planting movements and organizations

United Nations Environmental Programme's One Billion Trees Campaign
(http://www.unep.org/billiontreecampaign)

The Greenbelt Movement (http://www.greenbeltmovement.org)

The Forest Stewardship Council (http://www.fsc.org)

World AgroForestry Centre (http://www.worldagroforestrycentre.org)

Walking the Talk

Tom Sisulak, a member of Riverside United Methodist Church in Riverside, Illinois, asked his congregation to join him in an effort to keep local tree populations from disappearing in their town. His pastor and the whole congregation enthusiastically supported this "1,000 Tree Planting Project" in order to repopulate the once-forested area near the river, which had been losing trees. Over a period of months, Sisulak collected acorns and other seeds that had fallen from trees native to Illinois (northern red oak, bur oak, black walnut, and hickory). Volunteers helped him plant the trees. Even taking into account that for every six or eight seeds only one might survive, the project was a success, both for the actual forest it would help maintain but also for the community building it brought about and for the growth in the community's commitment to care for God's creation.

Jon Kaplan, "'Johnny Appleseed' Organizes Tree Planting Project," United Methodist News Service, December 5, 2007, http://www.umc.org/site/apps/nlnet/content3.aspx?c=lwL4KnN1LtH&b=2433457&ct=4723531.

FAITH MATTERS

For you shall go out in joy, and be led back in peace; the mountains and the hills before you shall burst into song, and all the trees of the field shall clap their hands.

ISAIAH 55:12

WILDERNESS AND LAND

In order to protect wilderness areas, we need first to know what land is already protected as well as what zoning laws and plans for future development leave other areas vulnerable. Most urban dwellers appreciate their city parks but realize that these often lack native plants, true habitat for wildlife, or any hint of real wilderness. People in many rural communities love their landscapes, only to find empty stretches of land quickly being turned into commercial areas. While not all development is negative, it is important that everyone in the community be allowed to participate thoughtfully in decisions about what they hope future landscapes will be. Whether in cities or rural areas, thoughtful decisions about local land use are crucial to protecting wilderness.

How To's

1 Find out from your city or town council what zoning laws exist and what areas are protected as either "green space" or wilderness areas. Ask what areas are slated for commercial development that currently are wilderness. What kinds of limitations on future development do wilderness protections offer?

2 Consider what restrictions you think are fair to put on the land. For instance, you may consider it just and appropriate to include native hunting or fishing rights in the wilderness areas on which indigenous communities have long depended for food.

3 Learn if local conservation groups have projects to reclaim any abandoned or unused industrial or commercial sites. How will they do the reclamation? What will they plant?

4 Host an old-fashioned storytelling night in your neighborhood or congregation to exchange memories and stories about your bioregion, sharing your favorite wild places (past or present).

Walking the Talk

While it is not Milwaukee's policy generally to sell vacant land to nonprofit organizations, a local church is interested in buying some empty lots in order to turn them into gardens. All Saints (ELCA) Church has begun a program to allow the neighborhood, which consists primarily of renters, to use and prosper from a garden on church land. The project has become popular enough that the church wishes to expand it and thus is engaging in efforts to purchase more vacant lots. In the meantime, members are "claiming lots as 'sacred ground' and tending them on their own."

"Fresh Food for All," available at http://www.nccecojustice.org/realstoriesgreatgreen.html.

FAITH MATTERS

A voice cries out: "In the wilderness prepare the way of the Holy One, make straight in the desert a highway for our God."

ISAIAH 40:3

Make Space for More Green

Before the Industrial Revolution, the notion that future generations might need to actively make space for wilderness to have a rightful place alongside human development might have been considered absurd. However, we have now reached a point where such green spaces are shrinking. Reclaiming current land for wilderness absorbs carbon dioxide, provides habitat for wildlife, and inspires people to care about creation. Creating more green spaces in urban areas in particular can create peaceful settings, lessen stress, and help keep city-dwellers connected to the rest of creation. Rural areas naturally have more green space, but it is worth investigating if there are some areas needing to be reclaimed.

How To's

1 **Find old parking lots or pavement** that can be turned back into grassy areas or gardens.

2 **Beautify current areas** that often go unattended or unnoticed. Search on the Internet for "guerrilla gardeners" to read about volunteer gardeners who beautify public spaces that have been neglected.

3 **Plant a garden on a flat rooftop** to absorb carbon emissions, keep the building insulated, and add color and life to an otherwise dull area.

4 **Encourage your town or city council to create a "green belt"** around the city—places that will be preserved from future development. Having a policy on the books is a necessary protection to keep and make green space.

5 **Explore ways to further the current protection of green spaces**— be they parks, meadows, forests, or prairies. Check with your local conservation organizations for ideas.

6 **Encourage gardeners and farmers to let some land lie fallow and/ or to plant cover crops** in the winter to enrich and protect the soil and encourage biodiversity.

7 **Volunteer as part of National Public Lands Day** each September. To learn more, go to http://www.publiclandsday.org.

Walking the Talk

In 2006, environmentally concerned students at Macalaster College helped create a green roof on top of the "Fishbowl," a passage between two student dorms. They researched the idea and found that it would slow water runoff, increase the building's insulation, absorb some of the "urban heat island" effect, and be a beautiful addition to campus. These college students are part of a larger movement to find ways to bring green space back into urban areas, housing developments, and school campuses.

Macalaster College's First Green Roof: A Presentation by Alese Colehour and Ellie Rogers, http://www.macalester .edu/environmentalstudies/students/projects/macalestersfirstgreenroof.pdf, and Rebecca Barnes-Davies and Jenny Holmes, "Living Lightly on God's Creation," *Presbyterians Today*, May 2007, http://www.pcusa.org/today/ cover/2007/cover0507.htm.

FAITH MATTERS

The land shall not be sold in perpetuity, for the land is mine; with me you are but aliens and tenants. Throughout the land that you hold, you shall provide for the redemption of the land.

LEVITICUS 25:23–24

Purchase Products That Protect Wilderness

It is easy to walk into a store and buy a brand-new wooden bookcase, a ream of office paper, or a pound of coffee without considering what impact that purchase has on wilderness areas (and, in the end, on climate change). However, these types of purchases are part of our personal pledge to care for the earth. The good news is that it is possible to buy products that protect wilderness no matter what income bracket we are in. Secondhand items are actually the best purchases, as they mean no additional resources were used and no extra energy consumed in order to produce the item that is new to you. However, for those who want a brand-new item (or need it, in the case of food products, for instance), opportunities abound to purchase fairly traded, sustainably harvested, high-quality products.

How To's

 1 When shopping for products made of wood, **try to buy secondhand.** Know your local consignment stores and yard sale schedules and you will be amazed at the products you can find for reasonable prices. If you can't find what you are looking for secondhand, look for wood that is certified by the Forest Stewardship Council (FSC).

 2 For home and office use, **buy recycled paper or paper that is certified by the FSC.**

3 **Drink fair-trade, shade-grown coffee.** Shade trees, among which coffee plants are grown, offer habitat for birds and add diversity to the soil. Drink fairly traded coffee that is shade-grown and helps to protect wilderness, whereas traditional coffee plantations clear the land of all trees.

4 For your church, **purchase "eco-palms"** for Palm Sunday (see "Walking the Talk" below).

Walking the Talk

Lutheran World Relief, Catholic Relief Services, the University of Minnesota, and the Presbyterian Church (U.S.A.) have all worked in recent years to promote the use of "eco-palms." Traditional methods of harvesting palms are harsh on forests as well as local laborers. These sustainably harvested palms, ordered by congregations for Palm Sunday, provide much more economic support to the palm harvesters than they would otherwise receive. The palms are also gathered in an environmentally sustainable way. Presbyterian staffperson Melanie Hardison comments, "A primary benefit of eco-palms is that they provide a nontimber source of income so that fewer hardwoods are cut in the forests where the chamadorea palms grow. These forests are part of sensitive bioregions in Central America, and some are found within biosphere reserves." All the way around, these palms echo the jubilation felt by Christian communities during Palm Sunday. To find out more or to buy eco-palms, see http://www.lwr.org/palms/index.asp.

FAITH MATTERS

If you treat gold like dust, and gold of Ophir like the stones of the torrent-bed, and if the Almighty is your gold and your precious silver, then you will delight yourself in the Almighty, and lift up your face to God.

JOB 22:24–26

Treasure the Globe's Wild Places

All around the world are magnificent landscapes, ecosystems, and natural wonders. The Great Barrier Reef, the Grand Canyon, the Galapagos Islands, Victoria Falls, Mount Everest, the Northern Lights, and many more amazing, complex, and beautiful parts of God's creation can inspire awe and encourage us to protect the earth for future generations. While we may not all be able to travel to these and other "natural wonders of the world," we can learn about them and be thankful for them. Wild places around the world are treasures whether they're internationally recognized or not. Whether traveling internationally or learning about wild places at home, the more we learn about the wild variety of God's creation, the better we can protect it.

How To's

1 Do a library or Internet search for natural wonders of the world. Learn about the wonders named by various authorities (there is no definitive list). Which inspire you? What do they have to teach us? How is God glorified in them?

2 Explore ways these areas are currently protected and if there are ways that they are threatened by human development and/or climate change.

3 Host a film fest or movie night in your church or home to learn about wild places around the world. Borrow videos from the library or local conservation groups, or rent them from video stores.

4 If you are planning a vacation, consider eco-tourism. Plan a trip to a natural wonder, a national park, or a little-known wild place. Bring home stories and pictures to share with your neighbors, family, or congregation.

Walking the Talk

Vineyard Christian Fellowship in Boise, Idaho, focuses on caring for wild places through its "Tending the Garden" ministry. Beyond doing education in the congregation and hosting environmental stewardship conferences, members of this congregation go into the wild to help care for God's creation. Vineyard Boise does trail maintenance in nearby national parks and offers wilderness retreats for families and individuals. The church's Web site explains, "Any type of stewardship requires servant-hood. As Christians, we will serve our community and the State of Idaho through volunteer work. We will clean up state campgrounds, reconstruct and maintain backcountry trails, clean up rivers, participate in wildlife inventories, and join other activities where service is needed to improve our environment."

The quotation is from http://www.letstendthegarden.org/positions/dirt1.htm. General information is from the church's Web site (http://www.letstendthegarden.org) and the Web site of the National Council of Churches' Eco-Justice Program (http://www.nccecojustice.org/wildmodels.htm).

FAITH MATTERS

God has not left God's self without a witness in doing good—giving you rains from heaven and fruitful seasons, and filling you with food and your hearts with joy.

ACTS 14:17

Leave No Trace

We humans like to leave our mark. Perhaps it is our animal instinct coming out. However, where many animals mark their territory with smell, we tend to mark what we think is our territory in much more indelible ways. We usually know humans have been there if something drastic has changed the landscape. Huge structures, changes in the natural course of a river, a forest that has been clear-cut—these are ways to tell humans have been through a particular part of God's creation. Is this the best way for us to be who God created us to be? Leaving no harmful trace of ourselves when we have walked through the woods or otherwise enjoyed the wilderness is one way to begin to walk humbly with God and to be helpful participants in God's creation.

How To's

1 **Follow wilderness rules of leaving no trace when exploring.** Carry out whatever you carried in.

2 **Study Scripture references to humility and to our place in covenant with God.** Recognize the arrogance embedded in the attitude that it is okay to leave visible marks of our presence.

3 **Take responsibility for proper disposal of your own trash, compost, recyclables, and toxins.** Understand that our waste, whether we live in cities or rural areas, impacts wild lands.

4 **Be cautious and thoughtful of new human inventions,** be they time-saving devices or new technologies. Insist that the burden of proof be on the new invention to prove it does not negatively harm creation before it is adopted.

Walking the Talk

Greg Hitzhusen, the executive director for Ohio Interfaith Power and Light, has long written and taught about the value of wilderness in Christian faith development. However, he doesn't just write and teach these things indoors. He takes trips himself into the wilderness and knows the value of leaving no trace. He explains, "Growing up, I enjoyed the triple delights of gardening, camping, and wilderness backpacking. I think that each one of us, as a human made from the humus—an adam from the adamah, as it says in Genesis—has an innate connection with the land, such that by caring for the land, we also care for ourselves and for future generations. Leaving no trace in the wilderness is our way of preserving the natural abundance and beauty of wild lands; leaving no trace in our spiritual lives is having gratitude for the gift of life and giving our praise back to God for all the good things God has made. Leaving no trace allows the chorus of all creation to praise God without diminishment from human violence; once we have mastered the art of leaving no trace, we can advance to the craft of blessing God's good creation with our love and care. We can, after all, leave a good trace. As God blesses us, our path out of the wilderness leads to renewal and redemption in the world."

FAITH MATTERS

I brought you into a plentiful land to eat its fruits and its good things. But when you entered you defiled my land, and made my heritage an abomination.

JEREMIAH 2:7

It is important to get outdoors even if you can't get away from your neighborhood. Spending time outdoors is another way to connect to the wilderness, if on a more subtle scale. Dandelions pushing through concrete can teach the resilience of wild things. Swinging at the local park can be a way for a child to feel the pull of earth's gravity, the delight of wind, and the scale of human feet compared to tall trees nearby. While air pollution and high ozone days mean that there are times when it may be appropriate to stay indoors, we all can find some opportunities to get outside and enjoy the world outside our doorstep.

How To's

1 **Exit your front door,** knowing that God's creation is all around us even in urban areas or very domesticated rural areas.

2 **Realize that outdoor meals, playground time, neighborhood walks, and sports played on the lawn are all part of enjoying the outdoors,** exposing our senses to the wider world, and creating empathy with nonhuman life.

3 **Take a walk without talking.** Instead of human conversation, spend time on noticing beautiful flowers, interesting insects, and fascinating animal behavior or plant life.

4 **Pray for the world on your doorstep.** Sitting on your front porch, stairs, or balcony, pray to God in thanks for each thing you look upon, asking God's blessing on its life.

5 **Make up games,** such as versions of tag, that encourage participants to name parts of nature around them.

Walking the Talk

At Sunnyvale Presbyterian Church in California, Rev. Steve Harrington leads outdoor trips for fun and fellowship and for increasing appreciation of the beauty in the outdoors. Church members experience wilderness in some farther away locations as they kayak, canoe, or go on pilgrimage to the desert. However, they also make time for day trips—hiking, rock climbing, exploring—to appreciate the outdoors in places closer to home.

FAITH MATTERS

The earth is satisfied with the fruit of your work.

PSALM 104:13

8. LIVE

JUBILEE!

We are not in charge of the earth. We are not, by our own human prerogative, going to be able to save the world. We do not know enough. We do not have enough power or resources.

While these truths may make us nervous, they also can liberate us. As people of faith, we trust that God is already at work in the world, constantly moving the world toward good. Because God is omnipresent and active, we participate in the call to curb climate change knowing that we are not alone. We participate because it is a way to praise God, to honor the creation God made, and to become who we are called to be.

Humbly, thankfully, and respectfully, then, we engage in this awesome work. We learn not just what to do in the world but also how to be in the world. We learn what attitudes are appropriate to embody and what our human limits are. We take breaks when we need to rest. We cease activity if it is harmful to those most vulnerable in creation. We take time apart from the world, knowing that we must be filled by God before we can fill any need in the world. We benefit from jubilee just as all creation does.

LEVITICUS 25:10–12

And you shall hallow the fiftieth year and you shall proclaim liberty throughout the land to all its inhabitants. It shall be a jubilee for you: you shall return, every one of you, to your property and every one of you to your family. That fiftieth year shall be a jubilee for you. . . . It shall be holy to you.

CONCLUSIONS

God wants us to do good, not evil.

Revenge is a harmful thing.

Do not take revenge!

CASE CLOSED

Detective Dan

QUESTIONS TO EXPLORE AND ANSWER:

✔ Why did Farley take revenge?

✔ Was it a good reason?

✔ Did taking revenge make things better?

✔ What does the Bible say about revenge?

✔ Have you ever taken revenge?

✔ What happened?

SPECIAL NOTES TO REMEMBER:

What Revenge Does:

✔ It makes you act before you think.

✔ It makes you want to do evil.

✔ It may anger or hurt someone.

✔ It makes you do what you will be sorry for later.

When You Want to Take Revenge:

STOP! Think about what you are doing.

PRAY! Ask God to help you do what is good not evil.

FORGIVE! Forgive anyone who has
done something bad to you.

THE FLYING FROG
CASE WRAP-UP REPORT

VERSE OF THE WEEK:

"Do not repay anyone evil for evil.

Be careful to do what is right in the eyes of

everyone."

Romans 12:17

THE CULPRIT: REVENGE

Revenge is when you do something bad

to someone because they did

something bad to you.

LEARN TO READ

DETECTIVE DAN

and the

Flying Frog Mystery

written and illustrated by

Timothy Roland

ZondervanPublishingHouse
Grand Rapids, Michigan
A Division of HarperCollinsPublishers

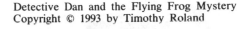

Requests for information should be addressed to:
Zondervan Publishing House
Grand Rapids, Michigan 49530

Library of Congress Cataloging-in-Publication Data

Roland, Timothy.
    Detective Dan and the flying frog mystery / Timothy Roland.
        p. cm.
    Summary: Detective Dan finds Farley's missing frog and, with the
aid of a Bible verse, helps him understand why seeking revenge is
wrong.
    ISBN 0-310-38121-5 (pbk.)
    [1. Frogs—Fiction. 2. Revenge—Fiction. 3. Christian life—
Fiction. 4. Mystery and detective stories.] I. Title.
PZ7.R6433Dc   1993
[E]–dc20   93-3498
                                                                    CIP
                                                                     AC

Edited by Dave Lambert and Leslie Kimmelman
Interior and cover design by Steven M. Scott
Illustrations by Timothy Roland

Printed in the United States of America

93 94 95 96 97 98 / CH / 10 9 8 7 6 5 4 3 2 1

To my brothers and sister:
Tom, Sue, Pete, Jon

CONTENTS

Chapter One
THE FLYING FROG

I am Detective Dan.

I like to solve mysteries.

But it is hard work.

One day I was resting
in my back yard
from all my hard work.
I looked at my Bible verse
for the week.

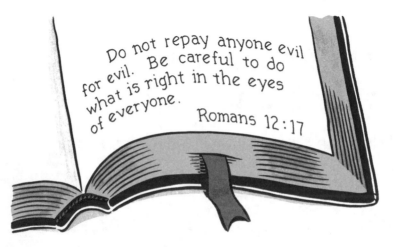

Do not repay anyone evil
for evil. Be careful to do
what is right in the eyes
of everyone.
Romans 12:17

It was a hard verse.
What did it mean?
Just then I heard the bushes shake.
I turned around.
My friend Farley came flying
through the air.

He landed next to me.

"You jump well," I said.

"So does my frog," said Farley.

"But he's missing!

Will you help me find him?"

"I am resting from

all my hard work," I told him.

"Why don't you just

catch another frog?"

"Because my missing frog

is special," Farley answered.

"Special?" I asked.

"My frog can jump very high,"
Farley explained.

"He looks like he is flying.

That's why I named him Jet."

I had never seen a flying frog before.
So I, Detective Dan,
decided to take the case.

"Tell me more
about your frog," I said.
"I was going to enter Jet in the
frog-jumping contest," Farley began.
"And he would have won!"
"Maybe someone took him," I said.
Farley smacked
his hands together.
"When I find them,
I'll get even!"
he yelled.
I looked at Farley.
My verse of the week
had warned about getting even.
But I could not worry
about that now.
I had a case to solve.

I grabbed my detective coat.

"Where did you keep Jet?" I asked.

"I will show you," said Farley.

He jumped over the bush.

I walked around it

and followed Farley.

Newton, my dog, followed me.

"Where are we going?" I asked.

"To my house," answered Farley.

I was puzzled.

"Isn't this the wrong way?" I asked.

"It's a shortcut," Farley said.

We soon arrived at a stream.

"What's that noise?" I asked.

"Frogs," answered Farley.

"They sound like
they're laughing," I said.
"They're happy because this is
their home," Farley explained.
"I caught Jet next to that fallen log."
"Does Jet have any special marks?"
I asked.
"Yes," answered Farley.
"There's a large dark spot
on his back.
It's shaped like a triangle."

14

I looked at a fallen log.

Something next to it moved.

It was Tara's brother, Jasper.

He was holding a paper bag.

He jumped up and ran.

Farley did not see him.

"Come on! Let's get to my house,"
Farley said.

He stepped across the stream
on some rocks.

Soon he was on the other side.

I tried to follow.

My foot slipped.

Splash!

Farley laughed.

So did the frogs.

I did not.

I, Detective Dan, was on a case.

And it was a wet one.

Chapter Two
FROG-IN-A-BOX

I followed Farley to his house.

He showed me a large box

in his back yard.

On top was a screen.

Something jumped.

I looked inside.

"Your frog is not missing," I said.

"I had two frogs," explained Farley.

"Flounder is still here.

But Jet is missing."

Flounder jumped again.

He hit the screen.

"Maybe Jet jumped and knocked
the screen off," I said.

"And then he escaped."

"The screen is too heavy,"
said Farley.

I picked up the screen.

Farley was right.

No frog could knock it off.

"When did you last see Jet?"

I asked.

"This morning," answered Farley.

 "We were practicing his jumps right before the Scratch attack."

"The what?"

"The attack by Tara's cat, Scratch,"

Farley told me.

Newton started shaking.

He was afraid of Scratch.

So was I.

"Tell me what happened," I said.

"I was in the back yard,"
said Farley.

"Suddenly, Scratch ran toward me.
She looked crazy."

"What did you do?" I asked.

"I ran into my house,"
answered Farley.

"To get away?" I said.

"No," Farley told me.

"To get my slingshot.
Tara and Scratch scared me.
So I was going to scare them back."

"Did you?" I asked.

"No. They were running away when
I came outside," said Farley.
"I chased them.
But I could not catch them."
"Did they have Jet?" I asked.
"I don't know," Farley answered.
"But when I got back to my house,
Jet was not in his box.
He was missing!"

Farley smacked his hands
together again.
"I will get revenge," he promised.
He pulled his slingshot
from his pocket.

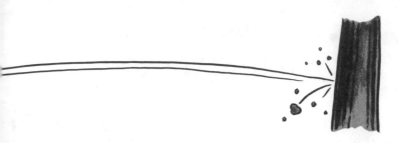

He shot a piece of dirt into a tree.
I remembered
my Bible verse.
Farley wanted
to pay back
evil for evil.
It was making
him act crazy.
I was worried.
And I needed
some answers.
I was on a case.
And it was a messy one.

Chapter Three
SCAREDY-CAT FROG

I walked toward Tara's house.

Suddenly, Newton barked.

I looked down.

I saw frog footprints.

They led to a high fence.

Then they stopped.

A frog could not jump
over that fence, I thought.
Unless he could fly, like Jet.
I climbed the fence.
Newton watched through a hole.
I saw Bernard.
He was holding
a string.
Tied to the
other end
of the string
was a frog.

27

"What's the string for?" I asked.

"To keep my frog
from jumping away," said Bernard.

"He's full of energy."

Bernard fed the frog a gumdrop.

The frog didn't look
full of energy.

He looked
full of fat.

"I'm training my frog to jump
over the fence," explained Bernard.
"Frogs can't jump that high,"
I told him.
Bernard said,
"I saw one do it this morning."
"Really?" I asked.
"Which way did he go?"

Bernard pointed toward

Tara's house.

I ran to the house.

Newton ran behind me.

Jasper was in the front yard.

He was still holding the paper bag.

"Is your sister home?" I asked.

"No," said Jasper.

"Do you know where she is?" I asked.

"No."

Jasper's bag wiggled.

"What do you have in there?"

I asked.

"It's mine!" yelled Jasper.

"Is it a frog?" I said.

Jasper ran toward the bushes.

He crawled underneath.

I peeked over the top.

Jasper opened his bag.

I crossed my fingers.

I hoped the missing frog was inside.

But out crawled a turtle.

So the case was still a mystery.

And I was running out of clues.

I walked slowly

toward Farley's house.

A frog jumped on the sidewalk

in front of me.

"Catch him!" yelled Farley.

I leaped toward the frog.

He leaped away.

I leaped again.

I closed my hands around the frog.

He wiggled.

"Nice going," said Farley.

"You caught Flounder."

"How did he get away?" I asked.

"I was exercising him

in the back yard," began Farley.

"Then I saw Tara and Scratch.
So I ran inside to get my slingshot."
"And you forgot about Flounder,"
I said.
Farley looked down at his frog.
"Yes," he answered. "I guess I was
more interested in getting revenge."
"That's it!" I said.
"A clue to help solve the case!"
"What clue?" asked Farley.

"This morning you
were exercising Jet," I answered.
"Then Scratch attacked.
You went to get revenge.
And you forgot to put Jet
back in his box."

Farley put his hands
on his head.
"That means
nobody took
him," he said.

"Not if I'm right," I agreed. "I think Jet was scared and hopped away."

"So how do we find him?" Farley asked.

It was a good question.

I just wished I had a good answer.

Chapter Four
FROG AT HOME

"Look," said Farley.

"Tara's going to my door."

He pulled out his slingshot.

He took a shot.

He hit the side of his house.

Scratch jumped
into the air
and then ran
through the bushes.
Tara turned
and faced Farley.
"What's the big idea?" she yelled.

"You could have
hit somebody!"
"It was just
a warning shot,"
said Farley.
"I just wanted
to scare you."

"Why?" asked Tara.
Farley explained. "Because this
morning Scratch tried to scare me."

Tara laughed.

Farley crossed his arms.

"What's so funny?" he asked.

"Scratch was stung by a bee,"
said Tara. "That's what
made her go crazy."

She pointed toward the bushes.

"There's a beehive in there,"
she said.

"I came back to warn you about it."
Farley's face turned red.

"I guess I tried to get even with you
and Scratch for nothing," he said.

"I'm sorry."

"Where is Scratch?" I asked.

"She probably ran home," said Tara.

"She always goes there
when she's scared."

"That's it!" I said.

"That's what?"
asked Farley.

"That's where your
missing frog is.
Follow me," I said.

I walked to the stream.
I looked near the old log.
A frog jumped.
On its back was a spot
shaped like a triangle.

"That's Jet!" yelled Farley.
"But how did you know
he was here?"
"He was scared this morning,"
I said. "So he headed home.

And this is his home."

Jet jumped across the stream.

"Now we have to catch him,"
said Farley.

"You mean you have to catch him,"
I said. "I agreed to help find him,
not to catch him. And he is found.
So the case is over."

I smiled.

Farley leaped toward Jet.

I hoped Farley would catch his frog.

I also hoped

he would stop taking revenge.

Revenge makes

detective work harder.

I was tired.

Newton was too.

So I did not wait for Farley

to catch his frog.

I carried Newton home.

And we rested up for our next case.